MW01073268

"This isn't a GPS-plotted route to beco[m]
better, more like a Fodor's travel guid[e]
decide whether and where you want to go, then provides first-class
advice on optional routes, preparations for the trip, and how to manage
the bumps and detours on the way."
– Thomas Grisso, University of Massachusetts
Medical School, USA

"To those contemplating a career in forensic psychology, the pathway is
often not clear. Understanding and navigating undergraduate preparation, graduate school applications, graduate training, the internship
application process and experience, licensure, and various aspects of
one's early career experience is challenging. DeMatteo and his colleagues
have provided the perfect roadmap. They answer most, if not all, of the
questions many have about these matters, and they provide strategies that
maximize one's chances for success at each step in the process. For each
topical area, the authors identify key factors readers should consider as
they go about the decision-making process."
– Randy Otto, University of South Florida, USA

"The field of forensic psychology is both intriguing and captivating but
the path to becoming a forensic psychologist can be difficult to navigate.
In *Becoming a Forensic Psychologist*, DeMatteo, Fairfax-Columbo, and
Desai provide a masterful blueprint for pursuing a career in this field.
This important text is a 'must' for anyone considering a career in
forensic psychology."
– Patricia A. Zapf, Palo Alto University, USA

Becoming a Forensic Psychologist

The paths to becoming a forensic psychologist are numerous and varied. *Becoming a Forensic Psychologist* provides insight into the process of pursuing a career in forensic psychology, from an introduction to the field itself to graduate school and beyond.

This comprehensive guide extends beyond mere definitions and overviews to discuss tips, strategies, and questions to ask at every step of the way to becoming a forensic psychologist. Told from the perspectives of individuals at different stages in their career, this book provides up-to-date information about existing forensic psychology programs and resources to assist aspiring forensic psychologists in career decision-making. Additional sidebars define key terms, highlight important court decisions that shaped the field of forensic psychology, and provide interesting facts about the field.

This book will help any individual pursuing a career as a forensic psychologist, including those about to start college who are narrowing their career interests, graduate students, and those already in the field of psychology who are considering a career shift.

David DeMatteo, JD, PhD, ABPP (Forensic), is an Associate Professor of Psychology and Law at Drexel University, and Director of Drexel's JD/PhD Program in Law and Psychology. He is board certified in forensic psychology by the American Board of Professional Psychology.

Jaymes Fairfax-Columbo, JD, PhD, is a graduate of the Thomas R. Kline School of Law and Drexel University's College of Arts and Sciences.

Alisha Desai, MS, is a doctoral candidate in the PhD Program in Clinical Psychology (forensic concentration) at Drexel University.

Becoming a Forensic Psychologist

David DeMatteo,
Jaymes Fairfax-Columbo,
and Alisha Desai

Routledge
Taylor & Francis Group

NEW YORK AND LONDON

First published 2020
by Routledge
52 Vanderbilt Avenue, New York, NY 10017

and by Routledge
2 Park Square, Milton Park, Abingdon, Oxon, OX14 4RN

Routledge is an imprint of the Taylor & Francis Group, an informa business

© 2020 Taylor & Francis

The right of David DeMatteo, Jaymes Fairfax-Columbo and Alisha Desai
to be identified as authors of this work has been asserted by them in
accordance with sections 77 and 78 of the Copyright, Designs and
Patents Act 1988.

Library of Congress Cataloging-in-Publication Data
A catalog record for this title has been requested

ISBN: 978-1-138-59537-8 (hbk)
ISBN: 978-1-138-59540-8 (pbk)
ISBN: 978-0-429-48830-6 (ebk)

Typeset in Bembo
by Swales & Willis, Exeter, Devon, UK

To Kirk Heilbrun, who taught me to be a forensic psychologist.
David DeMatteo

For my mother, Tina, my father, Russell, and my brother, Bryan, for providing me love and support over the years.
Jaymes Fairfax-Columbo

For my mother, father, and brother, from whom I continue to learn the value of dedication and of pursuing what you love. For John, whose support and companionship make all the difference.
Alisha Desai

To the next generation of forensic psychologists.
David DeMatteo, Jaymes Fairfax-Columbo, and Alisha Desai

Contents

Preface

The field of forensic psychology has grown considerably over the past several decades, and the application of psychological expertise in legal contexts is in higher demand than ever before. Attorneys and courts are increasingly relying on the expertise of forensic psychologists to address a range of legal questions in criminal and civil law contexts, while lawmakers, policymakers, and administrators are seeking psychological expertise to craft evidence-based policies and laws at historically high levels. Moreover, new training programs in forensic psychology are being developed with some regularity across the United States. Despite the continued growth and development of the field of forensic psychology, we noticed that information about how to become a forensic psychologist was not readily available, which is why we wrote this book.

We had two goals in mind when writing this book. First, by describing the many roles forensic psychologists can fulfill in clinical, research, academic, and consultation capacities, this book provides readers with a clear understanding of the specialized skills that forensic psychologists possess and the job contexts in which forensic psychologists can use those skills. Second, this book provides individuals interested in a career in forensic psychology with a straightforward blueprint for becoming a forensic psychologist. As you will see, there are various paths to becoming a forensic psychologist, and we outline multiple ways to pursue a career in forensic psychology.

This book is divided into three parts that roughly correspond to three major phases in the process of becoming a forensic psychologist. In Part I, we focus on helping you decide whether a career in forensic psychology is right for you. Chapter 1 provides an overview of the field of forensic psychology, the specialized skills forensic psychologists possess, the types of activities in which forensic psychologists engage, and the features that distinguish forensic psychologists from other types of psychologists. We also discuss the importance of having some understanding of the law given that forensic psychology is firmly at the intersection of psychology and law. In Chapter 2, we take a step back and provide a brief history of the field of forensic psychology, beginning with its origins and tracing its evolution to the present day. Understanding the history of forensic psychology will place the field in its proper context. Next, in Chapter 3, we provide foundational content for applying to graduate school, including the different types of forensic psychology graduate programs that are available, how to obtain research and work experience conducive to gaining admission to graduate school, the various prerequisites for applying to graduate school, and the concept of career specialization.

Part II encompasses the graduate school application process and graduate school itself. To that end, Chapter 4 focuses on preparing for the graduate application process, with a discussion of how to determine the type of degree and training program that would best fit your needs. In Chapter 5, we discuss the graduate school application process, providing insights on how best to maximize chances of acceptance and what to do in the event you are not accepted to graduate school. Chapter 6 focuses on how to survive and thrive in graduate school, and we address topics relating to getting involved in forensic research, choosing clinical practicum experiences, navigating professional conferences, publishing, networking, and self-care. We conclude Part II with Chapter 7, which focuses on navigating the internship process. In Chapter 7, we provide an overview of clinical internships, discuss how to determine which internship is the best fit, provide tips for maximizing your chances of obtaining an internship, and explain how the internship "match" process works.

Part III is focused on life post-graduation, with an emphasis on the range of opportunities in which early-career professional forensic psychologists might be interested. In Chapter 8, we discuss postdoctoral training opportunities, including how to decide if a postdoctoral fellowship is necessary, what type of postdoctoral fellowship to pursue, how to choose the postdoctoral program that offers the best fit, and other paths (including non-traditional paths) towards specialization in forensic psychology. Chapter 9 focuses on practice qualifications, including the process of becoming a licensed psychologist, obtaining board certification in forensic psychology, and the ethical and practice guidelines for forensic psychologists. Finally, Chapter 10 focuses on various types of jobs for forensic psychologists, and it explores other relevant considerations for early-career professionals, such as getting involved in professional organizations and keeping abreast of the latest developments in forensic psychology.

There are various ways to read this book. First, you can read this book in the traditional cover-to-cover way, which would provide the most comprehensive and sequentially logical information for becoming a forensic psychologist. Second, we designed this book so that each chapter can stand alone, which means you can choose to read the specific chapters that are most appropriate for you given your career status and interests. If you have not yet decided whether a career in forensic psychology is right for you, we recommend beginning with Chapter 1 and reading the chapters sequentially. If, however, you are already in graduate school and are looking for tips on maximizing your graduate school experience, or you are already in the field of psychology and looking to re-specialize as a forensic psychologist, some of the earlier chapters may not be as relevant.

Forensic psychology is an exciting and rapidly growing field that provides the opportunity to engage in meaningful work in a wide variety of clinical, research, academic, and legal settings. If you like the idea of working with individuals who are involved in the justice system, conducting research on topics that lie at the intersection of psychology and law, and helping legal decision-makers make better-informed decisions, then forensic psychology may be a great career choice for you. After reading this book, we hope you are as excited about forensic psychology as we are. Happy reading!

David DeMatteo
Jaymes Fairfax-Columbo
Alisha Desai
Philadelphia, PA

Part I

Career Crossroads

CHAPTER 1

Forensic Psychologists

What Exactly Do They Do?

WHAT IS FORENSIC PSYCHOLOGY?

If you are reading this book, then you probably want to become a forensic psychologist, or you are at least entertaining the idea of becoming a forensic psychologist. Some of you may always have had an interest in forensic psychology and are now seriously considering it as a career, while others may have just recently heard about forensic psychology from a television show, podcast, or movie. Regardless of how or when you became interested in forensic psychology, we can tell you that forensic psychology is an exciting field that is experiencing tremendous growth, and being a forensic psychologist offers the opportunity to engage in meaningful work in a variety of roles and settings.

If you are like most people, you may not be exactly sure what forensic psychologists do. When most people hear the phrase "forensic psychology," lots of images come to mind, many of which are probably not accurate. Despite being one of the fastest-growing specialty areas in psychology, there are many misconceptions about what forensic psychology is and what forensic psychologists do. Some people think forensic psychology has something to do with autopsies, while others think it involves criminal profiling or collecting evidence at a crime scene. If you want to become a forensic psychologist, or you *think* you might want to become a forensic psychologist, it is important that you understand what forensic psychology is and what forensic psychologists do (and do not do!).

The confusion surrounding forensic psychology most likely stems from how the term "forensic" is used in movies, television shows, books, and the media. Over the past several years, use of the term "forensic" has become commonplace and there are quite a few portrayals of professionals who are labeled "forensic psychologists" in movies, such as *Silence of the Lambs* and *Manhunter*, and television shows, including *CSI*, *Bones*, *Law and Order*, and *The Profiler*. References to forensic psychologists in books, news articles, and Internet blogs are also becoming much more common. The increasing attention paid to forensic psychology has generated interest in the field, but ultimately resulted in several misconceptions about the nature of forensic psychological work.

A wide variety of activities and professions can be considered forensic, so it is important that we begin our discussion of forensic psychology by first defining the term "forensic." The word "forensic" comes from the Latin word *forensis*, which is translated as "the forum." In ancient Rome, the forum was the public center of commercial, religious, economic, and political life. The forum was also where speeches and debates occurred (hence the use of the term "forensic" to describe some high school and college public speaking and debate clubs) and where legal trials took place.

In its current usage, the term "forensic" simply means that an activity or profession is related to the law or a legal process. Perhaps the most common usage of the term "forensic" is among forensic pathologists. Forensic pathologists, who are more commonly referred to as medical examiners, are physicians who specialize in conducting autopsies to determine the cause and manner of someone's death, typically when an individual has died suddenly, unexpectedly, or violently. This profession is "forensic" because determining the cause of someone's death is a legal question, and the results of the post-mortem examination are documented on a death certificate, which is a legal document.

Many other professions can also be considered forensic. For example, forensic accountants apply the practice of financial accounting in the context of actual, pending, or anticipated legal disputes. Forensic accountants, who are also called forensic auditors or investigative auditors, may provide evidence in a variety of legal contexts, including tax fraud, money laundering, valuation of a business entity, corporate mergers and acquisitions, the location of money in a contested divorce case, or economic damages in a personal injury case or contract dispute. Another example of a forensic profession is forensic odontology, which is the application of dental science to legal questions. In some contexts, forensic odontologists may assist law enforcement in the identification of criminal offenders by comparing a suspect's dental records to bite marks left on a victim, or they may identify human remains based on dental records. Incidentally, the serial killer Ted Bundy was ultimately convicted based on the testimony of a forensic odontologist.

Given the meaning of "forensic," we can state that forensic psychology is simply the application of psychology to the law. As discussed in more detail later in this chapter, there are numerous ways in which the science and practice of psychology can be applied in a variety of legal contexts (see Costanzo & Krauss, 2018). Although the definition of forensic psychology seems straightforward, there is considerable debate and disagreement – even among experienced forensic psychologists – about how broadly forensic psychology should be defined.

At a basic level and using a broad definition, forensic psychology can be conceptualized as the application of the science and practice of psychology to questions and issues relating to the law and the legal system. Using the broad definition of forensic psychology as a starting point, there has been vigorous debate regarding what activities and roles should appropriately be considered as falling within the province of forensic psychology (Brigham, 1999; DeMatteo, Marczyk, Krauss, & Burl, 2009; Neal, 2017; Otto & Heilbrun, 2002). A narrow definition of forensic psychology only includes the provision of clinical psychological expertise to individuals involved in the judicial system. Under this restrictive definition, only those psychologists who conduct evaluations or provide treatment in legal contexts would be considered forensic. This definition would include, for example, conducting evaluations of criminal defendants to see if they were insane at the time of the offense, evaluating someone injured in a car accident to see if they have "psychological damages," or providing restorative therapy to criminal offenders who have been found incompetent to stand trial. The problem with this narrow definition of forensic psychology is that it excludes psychologists who do not apply clinical skills, but instead conduct research in areas that are relevant to the law. As a result, researchers in areas such as social, experimental, cognitive, and developmental psychology would not be considered forensic psychologists under this narrow definition, even though the results of their research can significantly influence the legal system.

In this book, we endorse a broad definition of forensic psychology that is consistent with the definitions adopted by leading psychology and forensic psychology organizations. For example, the American Board of Forensic Psychology (ABFP), which is the premier advanced credentialing (board certification) organization for forensic psychologists in the United States, defines forensic psychology as the application of scientific, technical, or other specialized knowledge of psychology to inform matters within the judicial system, legislative bodies, and administrative agencies. Similar to the narrow definition of forensic psychology, the ABFP definition encompasses evaluations in legal contexts, but it also includes treatment and research activities that are conducted in anticipation of future legal, contractual, or administrative proceedings.

Another broad definition of forensic psychology was adopted by the American Psychological Association, the world's largest professional organization for psychology professionals and students. In the *Specialty Guidelines for Forensic Psychology*, which was adopted as official American Psychological Association policy in 2011, forensic psychology includes "professional practice by any psychologist working within any subdiscipline of psychology (e.g., clinical, developmental, social, cognitive) when applying the scientific, technical, or specialized knowledge of psychology to the law to assist in addressing legal, contractual, and administrative matters" (American Psychological Association, 2013, p. 7). This broad definition of forensic psychology encompasses clinical, research, and consultation activities, and it recognizes the widely varying roles that can be assumed by forensic psychologists in a variety of settings.

Consistent with the definitions of forensic psychology recognized by the ABFP and the American Psychological Association, we endorse a broad definition of forensic psychology that includes evaluations, treatment, research, and consultation activities that address some aspect of the law. This broad definition recognizes the contributions that can be made to various aspects of the United States legal system by psychologists working in clinical, research, and consultation capacities.

WHAT ISN'T FORENSIC PSYCHOLOGY?

Before moving forward with our discussion of forensic psychology, we should clarify what forensic psychology does *not* include. The two most common – and highly persistent! – myths surrounding forensic psychology are that forensic psychologists are involved in criminal profiling and the collection of crime scene evidence. In fact, many of the inquiries we receive from prospective forensic psychology students reflect their interest in becoming "an FBI profiler" or working with law enforcement to collect evidence at crime scenes.

Criminal profiling is a law enforcement investigative tool that helps to narrow down the pool of suspects following a crime. Based on their examination of the crime scene and other evidence, profilers provide a description – or profile – of likely suspects. Profiling is based on patterns and correlations observed in large datasets of crimes, criminal offenders, and crime victims. For example, if the victim of a homicide is Caucasian, statistics suggest that the offender is most likely also Caucasian. Profiling is an actuarial science, which means it is based on the application of statistical models. A non-forensic example of actuarial science is the differing rates that are charged for automobile insurance. Automobile insurance companies typically charge the highest premiums to young, single, male drivers because they are the most likely to have an automobile accident; based on large datasets of accident data, drivers who are young, single, and male have been "profiled" to be the highest-risk drivers.

As you can see, there is not much psychology involved in criminal profiling, although having knowledge of human thinking and behavior can be informative, and most psychologists are not involved in profiling. Although criminal profiling was once the exclusive domain of the Federal Bureau of Investigation (FBI; in the famed Behavioral Sciences Unit), local and state law enforcement agencies are increasingly utilizing criminal profilers. But these positions are filled by individuals who have extensive law enforcement experience, and psychological expertise is typically not a prerequisite for these positions.

The collection and processing of crime scene evidence, such as finger-prints, body tissues and fluids, and DNA specimens, is done by law enforcement professionals and other crime scene specialists. In television shows and movies, these individuals are often portrayed wearing police jackets with the word "forensic" prominently displayed on the back in large letters. Criminal evidence is referred to as forensic because it can potentially be used during a criminal investigation and the subsequent legal proceedings. It is certainly forensic science, but it is not forensic psychology.

WHAT DO FORENSIC PSYCHOLOGISTS DO?

Now that we have defined forensic psychology and discussed some activities that are not performed by forensic psychologists, we can briefly describe the types of activities performed by forensic psychologists. Using the broad conceptualization of forensic psychology, which is the application of the science and practice of psychology to questions and issues relating to the law, forensic psychologists can perform a variety of clinical, research, and consultation activities (Bartol & Bartol, 2018; Huss, 2014; Neal, 2017). In these contexts, forensic psychologists are using their expertise in the areas of human behavior, assessment of mental health functioning, treatments and interventions for mental health disorders, and the relationship between psychology and law to help inform legal decisions. We provide much more detail on the activities performed by forensic psychologists in Chapter 2.

FORENSIC PSYCHOLOGISTS VS. FORENSIC PSYCHIATRISTS

Now that we have cleared up the confusion regarding what forensic psychology is and what forensic psychologists do, we can address another point of confusion, which relates to the distinction between psychologists and psychiatrists and, by extension, the differences between forensic psychologists and forensic psychiatrists. Although there are many distinctions between these two professions, we focus on the three most prominent differences. First, psychiatrists are medically trained, with either a Doctor of Medicine (MD) degree or a Doctor of Osteopathy (DO) degree. By contrast, psychologists have non-medical doctoral degrees, typically a Doctor of Philosophy (PhD) or Doctor of Psychology (PsyD), although in some states and settings those with master's degrees can use the title "psychologist." This alphabet soup of advanced degrees is addressed more fully in Chapter 4. Second, the different training models of psychologists and psychiatrists are reflected in their practice. Clinical psychologists receive extensive training in the assessment and treatment of mental health disorders, whereas the training received by psychiatrists is focused largely on the treatment component, with a specific focus on the use of medications to treat mental health disorders. Finally, as medical practitioners, psychiatrists can prescribe medications, while psychologists generally are not trained or authorized to do so. With that said, psychologists have prescription privileges if they work in the United States military, and they have recently become eligible for limited prescription privileges in a few states (e.g., New Mexico, Louisiana), but prescription privileges for psychologists are the exception rather than the rule and obtaining such privileges requires a great deal of extra training.

When it comes to forensic work, psychologists and psychiatrists are generally involved in the same types of activities, with limited exceptions. Both forensic psychologists and forensic psychiatrists conduct mental health assessments of juveniles and adults in a range of criminal and civil law contexts. In some jurisdictions, there is a preference or even a legal requirement for psychiatrists to conduct certain types of forensic evaluations, most notably assessments of criminal offenders for competence to stand trial and insanity. The legal system has historically embraced the medical model of mental health disorders that is reflected in psychiatry, and some courts and attorneys have retained this bias in favor of forensic psychiatrists (see Slobogin, Hafemeister, Mossman, & Reisner, 2014). With that said, in most jurisdictions, psychologists and psychiatrists conduct the same types of forensic evaluations.

There are, of course, situations in which either a forensic psychologist or forensic psychiatrist may be preferred. Given their medical training, psychiatrists have greater expertise than psychologists in terms of medications, medical conditions, physiological functioning, and organic causes of mental health disorders, while psychologists typically have more extensive training in clinical assessment and multimodal interventions. There is, however, a more notable gap between the professions when it comes to research. Forensic research is typically conducted by psychologists (who, unlike psychiatrists, receive extensive research training while earning their PhDs), although some psychiatrists are prominent forensic researchers.

FORENSIC ASSESSMENT VS. TRADITIONAL CLINICAL ASSESSMENT

In this section, we focus on the role of forensic psychologists in conducting forensic mental health assessments of criminal offenders and civil litigants (see Heilbrun, DeMatteo, Brooks Holliday, & LaDuke, 2014). As previously noted, conducting forensic evaluations is the most common activity of forensic psychologists. Forensic evaluations include a range of assessments designed to assist legal decision-makers to make a decision (e.g., competence to stand trial, insanity, best interests of a child in a custody context), and we discuss many different types of forensic evaluations in Chapter 2. Clinical forensic psychology is most appropriately conceptualized as a specialty area within the broader parent field of clinical psychology. To become a clinical forensic psychologist, you first need to become a clinical psychologist (or a psychologist in a closely related field, such as counseling psychology; see Chapter 4 for a fuller discussion). Although forensic psychology (in terms of conducting forensic assessments) is subsumed under the broader field of clinical psychology, there are substantial differences between the two specialty areas.

If you asked a large group of laypeople to describe the first image that comes to mind when they hear the word "psychologist," most people would probably report picturing someone who provides therapy to distressed individuals. They might picture a psychologist taking notes in a nicely decorated office while the patient lies down on the stereotypical therapist's couch. That image is accurate in the sense that many psychologists focus on treating mental health disorders, but the image is very restrictive and not reflective of the many diverse roles played by other types of psychologists, including forensic psychologists.

The image of a "traditional" psychologist as a helping professional in a therapeutic context provides a useful comparison point for the role of forensic psychologists. The skills of a forensic psychologist are the same skills that are developed and used by clinical psychologists in traditional clinical settings, but a forensic psychologist's skills are applied in different ways to different populations and in much different contexts. In this section, we highlight the primary differences between evaluations conducted in a traditional clinical setting and evaluations conducted in a forensic context (see Heilbrun et al., 2014).

Purpose

The primary distinction between traditional clinical assessments and forensic assessments is the purpose of the evaluations. In a traditional clinical context, the purpose of the assessment is to diagnose mental health problems and develop a treatment plan. The patient's psychological well-being is the most important consideration, and psychologists are assuming the traditional helping role for which they are best known.

By contrast, in a forensic context, the purpose of the evaluation is to assist a legal decision-maker in making a decision about a criminal offender or civil litigant. The examinee's mental health functioning and treatment needs may be explored during the evaluation, but only if they are relevant to the legal question being addressed. The examinee's psychological well-being is not the primary consideration, and forensic psychologists are not assuming the traditional helping role.

Client

In a traditional clinical assessment, the client is the person being examined by the psychologist. But in a forensic context, the client is the person or entity that requested the evaluation, whether that is an attorney, the court, the examinee's employer, or the examinee's insurer. The key point is that the individual being examined in a forensic context is not the client. Identifying the client is not simply a matter of semantics; it has important implications for the obligations incurred by the psychologist, including the psychologist's duty to maintain confidentiality (which is addressed later in this chapter).

Relationship

Therapeutic relationships between a psychologist and patient are often characterized by empathy, support, and emotional safety. In a therapy context, psychologists seek to develop rapport with their patients, and they want their patients to feel comfortable sharing personal information. By contrast, in forensic contexts, psychologists typically strive to remain detached from the examinees (who are not the client), and the focus is more on obtaining complete and accurate information that is relevant to the legal question being addressed in the case. Also, although the forensic psychologist will, of course, act professionally, the relationship between the forensic psychologist and examinee is not typically marked by empathy and support.

Voluntariness and Autonomy

Most therapy relationships originate when someone seeks mental health treatment due to troubling symptoms, such as depression, anxiety, or drug abuse. Although an individual may feel pressured into seeking therapy, perhaps by a significant other, friend, or employer, in most cases the decision to enter therapy is ultimately voluntary and made by the patient. Because treatment is voluntary, the patient can withdraw from therapy at any time and for any reason, and typically without any negative consequences except perhaps the failure to resolve the problems for which the patient sought treatment. Moreover, because of the collaborative nature of the therapeutic relationship, the patient typically has greater input into the type of interventions that will be used by the psychologist, the goals of treatment, the length of treatment, and perhaps even the cost of the treatment.

By contrast, voluntariness and autonomy may not be present in forensic assessments. In forensic contexts, a court, employer, or insurer may require someone to undergo an evaluation, or their attorney may "strongly recommend" that they be evaluated. In many instances, there may be no available option for the examinee to decline participation, and the examinee can be forced to submit to the evaluation even if the evaluation could ultimately yield information that is unfavorable to the examinee's legal case.

Confidentiality

A patient in a traditional clinical relationship can expect that the psychologist will not disclose confidential information obtained during therapy (unless the psychologist is required by law to disclose certain information), but the examinee in a forensic assessment should not expect the information he or she provides to remain entirely confidential. Although forensic psychologists cannot recklessly disclose information they obtain during an evaluation, the results are shared with the attorney who requested the evaluation and often with the opposing attorney and court. In some cases, the forensic report may become part of the public record, which means that anyone with an interest in seeing the report could potentially obtain a copy of the report from the court.

Consent

In a traditional clinical context, the psychologist and patient share an understanding about the purpose of treatment. They both understand that the goal of the psychologist–patient relationship is to reduce the patient's clinical symptoms and improve his or her functioning. Obtaining informed consent (or the patient's agreement to participate in therapy) is a recommended practice for psychologists, but not something all psychologists do because there is an assumption that the patient is agreeing to participate in the therapy since the patient sought out treatment.

In a forensic context, the examinee's legal interests, including those relating to liberty/freedom and life, can be impacted by the results of the evaluation. The results of the forensic assessment could lead directly to a harsh criminal sentence, including incarceration or even a death sentence. Given what is often at stake in forensic assessment contexts, an examinee's understanding of key aspects of the evaluation, such as who requested the evaluation, the purpose of the evaluation, how the results of the evaluation will be used, and who will be able to see the report, may affect the examinee's willingness to participate in the evaluation or influence the types of answers the examinee provides during the interview and testing. If the forensic assessment is court-ordered, the examinee is required to participate, but if the evaluation is not court-ordered and instead simply requested by the examinee's attorney, the examinee must be given the opportunity to decline to participate in the evaluation.

Response Style

Patients entering therapy are typically not consciously motivated to conceal or distort the information they provide to a psychologist. Most patients recognize the importance of providing accurate information to assist the psychologist in developing a treatment plan, and they understand that therapy will be less effective if they are not honest. Therefore, in a clinical context, there is typically an assumption that the information provided by a patient is honest and reliable.

In contrast, involvement in legal proceedings may provide motivation for some people to hide or distort information. For example, criminal offenders may exaggerate symptoms of a mental health disorder to try to avoid going to trial or receiving a more severe sentence, or they may minimize any mental health symptoms they are experiencing because they believe it will help their case. In civil cases, a litigant may exaggerate mental health symptoms to obtain disability benefits or a large financial settlement after sustaining a personal injury, or a litigant may deny or minimize mental health symptoms to avoid the loss of liberty associated with involuntary psychiatric hospitalization. In the family law context, a parent in a child custody dispute may deny even minor psychological problems in an attempt to appear well adjusted and capable of parenting a child. Given the motivation for examinees to appear a certain way – either better or worse than they actually are – there is no assumption that examinees provide truthful information in a forensic assessment context.

Data Collection and Sources of Information

Traditional therapy relationships focus on patients' experiences, beliefs, and perceptions so the psychologist can understand how patients think, feel, and view themselves and their environment. Typically, the only source of information for a psychologist in a traditional therapeutic relationship is the patient, and it is rarely necessary to obtain information from additional sources.

In forensic contexts, however, the accuracy of information on which the forensic psychologist's conclusions are based is of fundamental importance, and corroboration of information obtained from the examinee is considered standard practice. Forensic psychologists routinely consider additional sources of information (besides the examinee), and they typically obtain additional information from the examinee's records (e.g., mental health, medical, criminal, school, employment) and individuals who are well acquainted with the examinee, such as significant others, employers, probation officers, physicians, teachers, and therapists.

Pace

Traditional clinical practice typically entails private, comfortable settings in which the relationship between the psychologist and patient develops naturally over time. The length of treatment may be determined in advance or open-ended (depending on the patient's symptoms and treatment goals), and the psychologist and patient can negotiate the frequency of treatment sessions, overall length of the treatment, and treatment goals. The psychologist and patient can often proceed at a clinical pace that is mutually comfortable, and there is typically no external pressure from third parties (except maybe insurance companies that may attempt to limit the number of sessions for which reimbursement is available).

In forensic contexts, evaluations are subject to deadlines imposed by the legal process. Due to impending court dates or procedural requirements, forensic psychologists may have limited time to conduct an evaluation. Criminal defendants have a constitutionally guaranteed right to a speedy trial, so delays in processing and adjudicating a defendant's case can result in the dismissal of the criminal charges. The deadlines inherent in forensic practice leave less time to develop rapport during the evaluation and to write the report.

Settings

Traditional therapy typically takes place in private, quiet settings, such as the psychologist's office or a patient's hospital room. The office may have a desk and a couch, perhaps with light music in the background, and a box of tissues in case the patient becomes emotional. By contrast, forensic assessments are often conducted in jails, prisons, or psychiatric hospitals that may offer little privacy and poor testing conditions.

Report

In a traditional clinical context, a written report (if created) is typically brief. Some evaluations conducted for a specific purpose may require a longer and more detailed report, such as when a student is evaluated for an Individualized Education Plan or when someone undergoes a lengthy neuropsychological test battery, but therapy progress notes are usually short and minimally detailed. Also, it is generally expected that no one other than the psychologist will ever see the progress reports.

In a forensic context, psychologists typically write lengthy and detailed reports that may be reviewed by attorneys, judges, and administrative bodies and entered into evidence in court and administrative proceedings. Reports in some contexts (e.g., child custody evaluations) can be 100+ pages. Also, the content of forensic reports differs from the content of traditional clinical reports. Whereas clinical reports focus on the patient's mental health functioning and perhaps a treatment plan, forensic reports focus on how the examinee's mental health functioning is related to the legal question being decided by the court.

Testimony

In a traditional therapy relationship, there is no expectation that the psychologist will provide expert testimony regarding the patient in a deposition, hearing, or trial. In fact, fulfilling two roles in the same case – such as being a treating psychologist and an expert witness – is contrary to psychologists' ethical guidelines because it can result in a conflict of interest (among other problems). However, in a forensic context, the psychologist should assume testimony will be required. In reality, forensic psychologists offer testimony in a small portion of their cases (perhaps 15–20%), but they should assume testimony may be needed and inform the examinee that testimony based on the evaluation is a potential outcome.

As you can see, there are many differences between evaluations conducted in a traditional clinical setting and evaluations conducted in a forensic context. We highlight the primary differences in Table 1.1.

Table 1.1 Differences Between Evaluations Conducted in Clinical Contexts and Forensic Contexts

	"Traditional" Psychologist	*Forensic Psychologist*
Purpose of evaluation	• Assessment, diagnosis, and treatment planning for mental health disorders	• Assist a legal decision-maker to make a more informed decision
Nature of standard(s) considered	• Medical (psychological, psychiatric)	• Medical (psychological, psychiatric) • Legal
Identity of the client, or for whom services are rendered	• Client and patient are usually one and the same, including instances in which the patient was referred to the psychologist by a third party	• Client is the party who requested the evaluation, not the person being examined • Evaluation is requested by an attorney, court, employer, or insurer

(Continued)

Table 1.1 (Cont.)

	"Traditional" Psychologist	Forensic Psychologist
Relationship between the professional and examinee	• Therapeutic alliance is cultivated • Psychologist assumes traditional "helping" role	• Objective or quasi-objective
Voluntariness of evaluation	• Relationship is typically initiated by the patient • Collaborative in nature	• Evaluations may be compelled by courts, employers, or insurers, or at the request of attorneys or courts
Confidentiality	• Typically limited to the psychologist–patient relationship unless the psychologist is required by law to disclose information	• Not limited to the forensic psychologist–examinee relationship; varies as a function of the client and the purpose of the evaluation
Requirement of obtaining informed consent	• Consent is implied by the patient having sought out the psychologist • Obtaining informed consent is recommended, but not something all psychologists do	• Because the examinee's legal interests are implicated, the examinee must be informed of who requested the evaluation, the purpose of the evaluation, how the results will be used, and limits on confidentiality • Formal and explicit consent (for voluntary participation) or notification of purpose (for involuntary participation) is necessary
Response style of examinee	• Because the evaluation is typically voluntary, the psychologist generally presumes patient responses are honest	• Because of the potential for secondary gain and the potential lack of voluntariness of the evaluation, there is an expectation the examinee may conceal or distort information • No presumption of reliable and truthful responses
Data collection	• Emphasis is placed on the patient's experiences, beliefs, feelings, etc.	• Emphasis is placed on the accuracy of information • Corroborating information via collateral documents

(Continued)

Table 1.1 (Cont.)

	"Traditional" Psychologist	Forensic Psychologist
	• Third-party or collateral sources of information may be helpful, but not always used	or third-party sources is expected practice
Sources of information	• Self-report • (Psychological testing) • (Behavioral assessment) • (Medical procedures) • (Records)	• Self-report • Psychological testing • Behavioral assessment • Observations by others • Relevant documents • Medical procedures • Collateral interviews
Setting	• Typically, a private office	• Settings vary widely and include correctional facilities, private offices, attorneys' offices, and forensic psychiatric hospitals
Pace	• Psychologist and patient can work collaboratively to negotiate frequency and duration of treatment	• Deadlines are imposed by the legal process • Less time is available for rapport building and report writing
Written report	• If a report is written, it is typically brief • Focus is on mental health or clinical functioning of the patient • No expectation anyone other than psychologist or patient will see the report	• Lengthy and detailed report is expected • Focus on functional legal capacities relevant to the legal issue being addressed • Expectation the report will be entered into evidence and potentially made part of the public records • Follow conventions/standards in forensic psychology
Expected outcome of the assessment	• Testimony is highly unlikely and, although it may be acceptable in limited circumstances, it is discouraged by ethical standards/guidelines	• Testimony should be anticipated as a possible follow-up to the evaluation and report

FORENSIC PSYCHOLOGY AND THE LAW

As previously noted, forensic mental health assessments are evaluations conducted by mental health professionals – typically psychologists, psychiatrists, and sometimes social workers – to assist a legal decision-maker to make a decision about a criminal offender or civil litigant. Forensic reports are submitted to attorneys, courts, and administrative boards in the context of a specific criminal or civil case. Forensic assessments are intended to facilitate better-informed legal decisions by a court or administrative board or to assist attorneys in their representation of a client.

All forensic assessments address a criminal or civil legal issue. In the criminal law domain, forensic assessments may address competence to stand trial, an offender's mental state at the time of the offense, state/federal sentencing, mitigation in the sentencing phase of death penalty cases, and many other legal questions. In the civil law domain, forensic assessments address, among other legal issues, competence to make medical/treatment decisions, the appropriateness of involuntary psychiatric hospitalization, the nature and extent of psychological damages, whether the court should appoint a guardian to oversee the needs of someone with a mental health disorder, and the best interests of children in a custody dispute. Given the nature of forensic assessments, it is perhaps obvious that forensic psychologists must have some familiarity with the laws that are relevant to the types of assessments they conduct.

The Importance of Understanding the Law

Because forensic mental health assessments address legal questions, forensic psychologists must have some understanding of the law (Roesch, Zapf, & Hart, 2010). But without the benefit of formal legal training, it can be difficult to understand laws and the legal system. After all, the law is full of arcane and technical language, complex and convoluted concepts, and unfamiliar rules and procedures. Although it is not necessary to receive formal legal training to become a forensic psychologist, it is important to have at least a minimal understanding of how the law works.

Having a sufficient understanding of the law makes a forensic psychologist better equipped to identify the forensic issue in a case, and this legal knowledge is then used to guide the forensic assessment. By specifying the forensic issues and abilities that are relevant to those issues, forensic psychologists can narrow the scope of an evaluation by asking questions and gathering data that are directly relevant to the legal issue. For example, in a competence to stand trial evaluation, a forensic psychologist with knowledge of the law knows to focus on the criminal offender's abilities to understand the nature of the criminal proceedings and assist the attorney in his or her own defense, which is how competence to stand trial is defined in most jurisdictions in the United States. Without knowing how a particular forensic issue is defined by the law, a forensic psychologist will not be able to conduct a meaningful evaluation or write a report that helps the court make an informed decision.

FORENSIC FUN FACT

For psychological evidence to be admitted in court, it must pass certain legal standards to ensure its reliability and accuracy. These legal standards vary by jurisdiction. Two common standards are the *Daubert* standard and the *Frye* standard. If a judge deems that the proffered evidence does not meet the relevant standard, the evidence cannot be admitted.

Besides informing and guiding the forensic assessment, knowledge of the law permits forensic psychologists to know which types of psychological tests will be accepted by a court. Judges make decisions about what types of evidence, including expert evidence (e.g., psychological tests), are acceptable in a specific case, and these decisions are guided by admissibility rules (or evidentiary standards). The rules that govern the admissibility of evidence differ by jurisdiction, so forensic psychologists must be familiar with the rules in their jurisdiction.

As illustrated above, forensic psychologists need some level of familiarity with the law, so in this section we provide a brief legal primer (see DeMatteo, Keesler, & Strohmaier, 2014, for a more detailed discussion of the law). After describing the various sources of laws in the United States, we present a brief overview of the structure of courts.

Sources of Law

What exactly does it mean to refer to "the law"? Where do laws come from and who makes the law? Is there some document or resource that lists all laws? Understanding the source of laws can be a surprisingly challenging process because laws come from a variety of sources and appear in various formats. Indeed, we know many 1L (or first-year) law students who struggle with understanding where laws come from.

As you may remember from your History or Government classes, the government is composed of three branches: legislative, judicial, and executive. The *legislative branch* creates statutes (a type of law explained later in this chapter), the *judicial branch* interprets those statutes in the context of specific disputes (which creates case law, another source of law discussed later), and the *executive branch* creates administrative agencies that carry out the law and enact regulations. In this section, we examine the various sources of law.

Primary Sources of Law

There are three primary sources of law in the United States: constitutions, statutes, and court cases. Constitutions provide specific rights and protections to all citizens. In the United States, all people are protected by both the U.S. Constitution and individual state constitutions. Constitutions afford rights and protect individuals largely by limiting governmental powers. Although many state constitutions closely parallel the U.S. Constitution, they may differ from the U.S. Constitution. State constitutions cannot provide less protection than the U.S. Constitution, but they can provide more protection.

Another primary source of laws is statutes. When many people envision what a law looks like, they may imagine some code or subsection with a potentially long string of letters and numbers, such as 18 USC § 2340A. Statutes are enacted by legislatures at the federal level (through Congress) or state level (through state legislatures), and they are often referred to as the law "on the books" or "black letter law." The statutes enacted by legislatures are compiled into books called the federal code and state codes. Other forms of statutes are enacted by local lawmaking authorities, such as city councils, and are typically called ordinances.

After a statute is enacted by a legislature, courts interpret and apply that statute in the context of specific disputes, which means the decisions made by courts are also a source of law. When applying the law, courts determine when and how the statute applies, whether there are exceptions to the application of the statute, whether the statute is consistent with the constitution, and several other decisions. A court can declare a statute invalid, which may require the statute to be revised by the legislature before it can be legally applied in another case. The interpretation of statutes across many cases results in a collection of judicial decisions referred to as case law (or common law). When judges are confronted with an issue that has previously been decided by another court, the judges may choose to follow this "legal precedent" by interpreting the law in the same way that the prior court interpreted the law. Alternatively, a court can choose to interpret the statute differently in a specific case, perhaps because the current case differs in some meaningful way from previously decided cases, which creates new case law.

Secondary Sources of Law

Constitutions, statutes, and court cases are considered primary sources of law because they effectively make the law in the United States. But there are also secondary sources of law, which can include anything that describes or summarizes the law. Common examples of secondary sources of law include *Black's Law Dictionary*, legal encyclopedias, and legal treatises (e.g., hornbooks, nutshells). Other secondary sources of law include books about the law sold online or at a bookstore, law review articles, legal newspapers or magazines, Internet articles and websites, and even podcasts or documentaries that focus on the law. Secondary sources of law can be helpful for those just starting to learn about the law because they are often aimed at people with no formal legal training.

Primary Sources of Law

Constitutions
Statutes
Court cases

Secondary Sources of Law

Black's Law Dictionary
Legal encyclopedias
Legal treatises
Law books

Structure of United States Courts

There are two major court systems in the United States: federal courts and state courts. Both the federal and state court systems can also be divided into criminal courts and civil courts. Each type of court hears specific types of cases. Federal courts hear matters governed by federal law (U.S. Constitution, federal statues, etc.), which includes crimes violating federal criminal law (criminal cases) and civil disputes arising between residents/entities of different states (or on certain legal issues that are reserved for federal courts by the U.S. Constitution) (civil cases). State courts hear matters governed by state law (state constitutions, state statutes, etc.), which include crimes that violate state criminal law (criminal cases) and civil disputes arising between residents/entities in the same state (civil cases).

Criminal Courts vs. Civil Courts

Criminal courts handle cases brought by the state or federal government against an individual who is alleged to have violated a criminal law. A crime is considered an offense against society, so the prosecutor (state or federal) is responsible for bringing criminal charges against a defendant on behalf of society. That is why criminal cases include the government as a party; for example, "*State of New Jersey* v. *Smith*" (state case) or "*United States* v. *Smith*" (federal case). Civil matters arise between two parties, so it is the responsibility of those parties to prove the case (plaintiff) and defend against the case (defendant). Because many legal questions fall under the province of civil law, civil courts are subdivided into various levels and the civil court system contains a variety of specialized courts, including family courts, probate courts, small claims courts, and landlord–tenant courts.

Jurisdiction

An important topic when discussing the different court systems and types of courts is jurisdiction, which is the authority of a court to decide a case. Jurisdiction is a complicated topic, and there are courses in some law schools dedicated exclusively to this topic. A few examples will illustrate the complexity. Murder is typically a state crime heard in state court, but if the murder victim is a federal employee (e.g., FBI agent, U.S. postal worker), the murder case would be decided in federal court. The location of the crime can also determine which court has jurisdiction. For example, possession of illicit drugs is typically a state crime heard in state court, but if someone commits a drug offense on federal property (e.g., Yosemite National Park), the perpetrator would be prosecuted in federal court. Finally, automobile theft is typically a state offense, but if the stolen car is federal property (e.g., U.S. mail truck) or the vehicle is driven across state lines, it would become a federal offense prosecuted in federal court.

Hierarchy of Courts

Within the federal and state court systems, courts are subdivided into hierarchies (or tiers). In the state court system, the first level of courts is the trial courts, which handle most criminal and civil cases. Trial courts determine the facts of the case and settle the dispute by applying the relevant law. Criminal trial courts apply penalties such as fines, judicially supervised release (e.g., probation), incarceration, and (in some jurisdictions) death, while civil trial courts apply penalties that are typically limited to monetary damages and injunctions (or an order for one party to stop engaging in certain behavior).

The next step up from trial courts is the intermediate appellate courts. These courts hear cases that have been appealed by one party from the trial court. If there are sufficient grounds to request that another court hear the case, such as when a trial court is alleged to have incorrectly applied the law, a party can appeal the case to the appellate court. Being eligible for an appeal does not guarantee that the appeal will be granted because appellate courts are not required to hear every case that is appealed. If the appellate court decides to hear the appeal, the court typically will not re-examine the facts of the case and will instead address whether the trial court applied the correct law in the correct manner in reaching its decision. If the appellate court determines that the trial court either applied the incorrect law or applied the correct law but in an incorrect manner, the appellate court can reverse the trial court's decision.

At the top of the hierarchy in the state court system is the state high court. Although this court is typically called the state supreme court (e.g., Pennsylvania Supreme Court, California Supreme Court), states have different names for their high court. In New York, for example, the highest court in the state is called the New York Court of Appeals; to complicate matters, the trial court in New York is called the New York Supreme Court. As with the intermediate appellate courts, state high courts have discretionary review and are not required to hear any cases. Typically, once the state high court rules on an issue, the decision is final, although it is possible that a case resolved at the state high court can be re-heard in a federal court.

In federal courts, the trial level court is called a district court, which functions like state trial courts in that they determine the facts of the case, apply the relevant law, and render a decision. There are 94 district courts spread out geographically across the United States and its territories. Federal district courts have general jurisdiction, which means they hear both criminal cases and civil cases.

There is also an appeals process in the federal court system. The intermediate federal appellate courts are known as the United States Circuit Courts of Appeal. There are 13 circuit courts in the United States, including 11 regional courts numbered 1 through 11 (e.g., United States Court of Appeals for the Tenth Circuit), the 12th Circuit for the

District of Columbia, and the Federal Circuit Court. Each circuit court has jurisdiction over a set number of the 94 district courts. For example, the United States Court of Appeals for the Third Circuit has jurisdiction over all district courts in Delaware, New Jersey, Pennsylvania, and the U.S. Virgin Islands.

At the top of the hierarchy in the federal court system is the Supreme Court of the United States. The Supreme Court consists of eight Associate Justices and one Chief Justice, and all justices are appointed by the President of the United States, confirmed by the Senate, and serve for life (until death, retirement, or impeachment). As a discretionary court, the Supreme Court typically only hears cases for which the Supreme Court justices have granted an appeal. Thousands of cases are appealed to the Supreme Court each year, but it only hears a small fraction (1–2%) of those cases. The Supreme Court has jurisdiction over all cases decided by federal circuit courts and all cases from state courts that implicate the U.S. Constitution or federal law. As the highest court in the United States, all decisions of the Supreme Court are final and cannot be heard by another court.

State Courts Hierarchy

High courts

↑

Appellate courts

↑

Trial courts

Federal Courts Hierarchy

Supreme Court of the United States

↑

U.S. Circuit Courts of Appeal

↑

U.S. District Courts

Binding Authority vs. Persuasive Authority

Having discussed the sources of law and how cases move through the state and federal court systems, it is important to understand the influence of a court's ruling. United States courts follow a system of *stare decisis*, which when roughly translated from Latin means to "maintain what has been decided and do not alter that which has been established." *Stare decisis* is alternatively referred to as a court's deference to precedent (previous decisions regarding the same/similar legal issues). Stated differently, when a judge faces an issue that has previously been decided by a court, the concept of *stare decisis* dictates that the judge follow the previous court's decision. In practice, however, the judge is not strictly required to follow the previous court's decision and can instead break from established precedent. The risk, of course, is that the judge's decision will be reversed on appeal because it departed from precedent. Whether a court is required to follow a previous court's decision hinges on the important distinction between binding authority and persuasive authority.

If the earlier ruling came from a higher court in the same jurisdiction, then a judge in that jurisdiction is required to follow the previous court's ruling. This is referred to as binding authority. For example, if the Supreme Court of Pennsylvania rules on an issue, lower courts in Pennsylvania are expected to follow the state supreme court's ruling. By contrast, a court reviewing decisions from a lower court in its jurisdiction or a court in another jurisdiction is not bound by the decisions of those other courts, although it may look to those other decisions for guidance. In that context, the way in which those other courts resolved the legal issue is viewed as persuasive authority.

One final point relates to the interplay between federal courts and state courts in terms of binding authority. All decisions by the U.S. Supreme Court are binding on all federal courts, but not all U.S. Supreme Court decisions are binding on state courts. The determining factor is whether the legal issue implicates state courts or only federal courts. For example, if the U.S. Supreme Court decides a case based on the U.S. Constitution, then all states are bound by that decision. But if the U.S. Supreme Court reaches a decision that is limited to federal courts – for example, how the Federal Rules of Evidence (which only apply in federal courts) should be interpreted – then the Supreme Court's decision does not affect state courts.

★ ★ ★

CONCLUSION

We hope this chapter has provided a solid foundation of what forensic psychology is and what forensic psychologists do. Having a sufficient understanding of the nature of forensic psychology is an obvious first step in deciding if forensic psychology is the right career choice for you. Later chapters will provide much more detailed information on the roles and activities of forensic psychologists.

REFERENCES

American Psychological Association. (2013). Specialty guidelines for forensic psychology. *American Psychologist, 68*, 7–19.

Bartol, C. R., & Bartol, A. M. (2018). *Introduction to forensic psychology: Research and application* (5th ed.). Thousand Oaks, CA: SAGE Publications.

Brigham, J. C. (1999). What is forensic psychology, anyway? *Law and Human Behavior, 23*, 273–298.

Costanzo, M., & Krauss, D. (2018). *Forensic and legal psychology: Psychological science applied to law* (3rd ed.). New York, NY: Worth Publishers.

DeMatteo, D., Keesler, M. E., & Strohmaier, H. (2014). Accessing the law and legal literature. In I. B. Weiner & R. K. Otto (Eds.), *The handbook of forensic psychology* (4th ed., pp. 57–83). Hoboken, NJ: John Wiley & Sons.

DeMatteo, D., Marczyk, G., Krauss, D. A., & Burl, J. (2009). Educational and training models in forensic psychology. *Training and Education in Professional Psychology, 3*, 184–191.

Heilbrun, K., DeMatteo, D., Brooks Holliday, S., & LaDuke, C. (Eds.). (2014). *Forensic mental health assessment: A casebook* (2nd ed.). New York, NY: Oxford University Press.

Huss, M. T. (2014). *Forensic psychology: Research, clinical practice, and applications* (2nd ed.). Hoboken, NJ: John Wiley & Sons.

Neal, T. M. S. (2017). Identifying the forensic psychologist role. In G. Pirelli, R. Beattey, & P. Zapf (Eds.), *The ethical practice of forensic psychology: A casebook* (pp. 1–17). Hoboken, NJ: Wiley.

Otto, R. K., & Heilbrun, K. (2002). The practice of forensic psychology: A look toward the future in light of the past. *American Psychologist, 57*, 5–18.

Roesch, R., Zapf, P. A., & Hart, S. D. (2010). *Forensic psychology and law.* Hoboken, NJ: John Wiley & Sons.

Slobogin, C., Hafemeister, T. L., Mossman, D., & Reisner, R. (2014). *Law and the mental health system: Civil and criminal aspects* (6th ed.). St. Paul, MN: West Publishing Co.

CHAPTER 2

Forensic Psychology

A Brief History and Current Status

To have a fuller understanding of forensic psychology, it is useful to examine how the field began and how it has developed over the years. The current practice of forensic psychology was heavily influenced by a number of key historical events, and having knowledge of those influential events will help place forensic psychology in its proper historical and current context. After presenting a brief history of the field of forensic psychology, this chapter describes the activities performed by forensic psychologists in current practice.

HISTORY OF FORENSIC PSYCHOLOGY

The relationship between psychology and law, which is at the core of forensic psychology, has a long history. The idea that someone's mental health should be taken into account when determining whether they should be held accountable for their actions can be traced back over 2,000 years to ancient Greek, Roman, and Hebrew civilizations. At that time, there were different views on the role mental illness should play in deciding whether someone should be punished for breaking the law. Although the philosopher Plato argued in 350 BC that mentally ill offenders (and their families) should be punished for their actions, Roman law recognized that offenders who were *non compos mentis* – or "not sound of mind" – should not be held accountable. The concept that the law should not punish people who are not aware of their wrongful actions, which is the basis of the modern-day insanity defense, is reflected in the Bible in Jesus's last words: "Father, forgive them for they know not what they do" (Luke 23:24).

Despite this long history, the roots of modern forensic psychology were established much more recently due to several key events in the late 1800s and early 1900s. The establishment of Wilhelm Wundt's psychology–law research laboratory in the late 1870s at the University of Leipzig in Germany was one such key event because it formalized the study of the relationship between psychology and law. Another major development occurred in the early 20th century with the publication of an influential book by a Harvard psychologist named Hugo Münsterberg. In 1908, Münsterberg published his treatise *On the Witness Stand*, which highlighted several areas of forensic psychology research, many of which are still of interest today (e.g., false confessions, eyewitness testimony). Another influential event was the development of William Healy's Chicago Juvenile Psychopathic Institute for the treatment of juveniles who committed crimes. As a result of Münsterberg's book and the work of other mental health professionals who advocated for the integration of psychology and law, mental health professionals became more integrated into the legal system in the early and mid-1900s. Around that time, mental health professionals began providing clinical services to adult and juvenile offenders, conducting psychological fitness testing of law enforcement personnel, and conducting evaluations of criminal offenders (Bartol & Bartol, 2018).

Several developments after World War II further contributed to the growth of forensic psychology in the United States. One key development was that social science briefs (sometimes called "Brandeis Briefs") were used in several important legal cases; these briefs are legal documents submitted to courts by people or organizations that are not part of the legal dispute for the purpose of helping the court make a better-informed decision. For example, in the landmark desegregation case *Brown* v. *Board of Education* (1954), the Supreme Court of the United States relied in part on psychological research summarized in a social science brief in concluding that racial segregation in schools was unconstitutional.

A significant development that promoted the growth of forensic psychology occurred in 1962 with the court case *Jenkins* v. *United States*. Throughout most of the legal system's history in both England and the United States, courts typically preferred the testimony of psychiatrists to that of psychologists when someone's mental health was at issue. This preference for psychiatrists was based on the law's acceptance of the medical (as opposed to psychological) model of mental illness. However, in *Jenkins*, the United States Court of Appeals for the District of Columbia Circuit ruled that properly trained and qualified psychologists could offer expert testimony on mental health disorders. The *Jenkins* ruling, which was adopted in most jurisdictions in the United States, opened the door for forensic psychologists to play a more prominent role in the legal system. The result was dramatic growth in the field of forensic psychology, and forensic psychologists now conduct many thousands of forensic mental health assessments each year on a variety of legal issues in criminal and civil courts (see Neal, 2017).

PROFESSIONAL ORGANIZATIONS FOR FORENSIC PSYCHOLOGY AND PSYCHIATRY

- American Academy of Psychiatry and the Law
- American Psychology-Law Society
- Australian and New Zealand Association of Psychiatry, Psychology and Law
- European Association of Psychology and Law
- International Academy of Law and Mental Health
- International Association for Correctional and Forensic Psychology
- International Association of Forensic Mental Health Services

Although the relationship between psychology and law dates back hundreds of years, the field of forensic psychology has experienced remarkable growth in the past several decades. For example, there are several national and international professional organizations devoted to forensic psychology (or the related field of forensic psychiatry). The American Psychology-Law Society (AP-LS) was founded in 1968 as forensic psychology's first professional association. Having once had less than 50 members, AP-LS currently has over 3,000 members (including a large portion of students) and is recognized as the most prominent professional group for forensic psychologists in the world (see Grisso & Brodsky, 2018).

EXAMPLES OF FORENSIC PSYCHOLOGY JOURNALS

- *Behavioral Sciences and the Law*
- *Criminal Justice and Behavior*
- *International Journal of Forensic Mental Health*
- *Journal of the American Academy of Psychiatry and the Law*
- *Journal of Interpersonal Violence*
- *Law and Human Behavior*
- *Psychology, Crime and Law*
- *Psychology, Public Policy, and Law*

Another indicator of the growth of forensic psychology is the increasing research and literature on forensic psychology topics. Forensic psychological research increased dramatically beginning in the mid-1970s, and there are currently numerous professional journals devoted to publishing empirical, theoretical, and practice articles relevant to forensic psychology.

DID YOU KNOW?

Oxford University Press publishes a series of books focused on best practices in forensic mental health assessment. Each book is authored or co-authored by some of the field's foremost experts. Currently, the series includes 19 books covering a wide variety of forensic topics.

There are also hundreds of books devoted to various aspects of forensic psychology. Some are more academic in nature and targeted to researchers and practitioners, including the Best Practices in Forensic Mental Health Assessment series published by Oxford University Press and a book series published by AP-LS, while other books on forensic psychology are mass marketed to the general public. Also, myriad television shows, movies, and podcasts relating to forensic practice attest to the growing popularity of forensic psychology among the general public.

Finally, the growth of forensic psychology is reflected in the recent proliferation of forensic psychology training programs and the development of board certification in forensic psychology (DeMatteo, Marczyk, Krauss, & Burl, 2009). Many colleges and universities are offering undergraduate courses in forensic psychology, and there are numerous graduate programs that provide some level of specialized training in forensic psychology for those interested in obtaining a master's degree, doctoral degree, or joint degrees in psychology and law (Burl, Shah, Filone, Foster, & DeMatteo, 2012). Further, many graduate internships, postdoctoral training programs, and continuing education seminars provide opportunities to work with forensic populations and receive advanced specialty training in forensic psychology. Finally, the American Psychological Association recognized forensic psychology as a discrete specialization area in 2001, and psychologists can obtain board certification in forensic psychology from the American Board of Professional Psychology. Available training programs are discussed in more detail in Chapter 4, forensic internships in Chapter 7, postdoctoral training programs in Chapter 8, and credentialing (licensure and board certification) in Chapter 9.

FORENSIC PSYCHOLOGY TODAY

The modern practice of forensic psychology was heavily influenced by its history, and the roles and activities of forensic psychologists in current practice stem largely from historical events that shaped the field. As mentioned in Chapter 1, forensic psychologists serve a variety of roles and perform a range of activities. As will be described, forensic psychologists can serve as forensic clinicians, forensic researchers, and forensic consultants in a variety of legal contexts.

Forensic Clinicians

Forensic Mental Health Assessments

Clinically based activities are perhaps the most well-known aspect of forensic psychology. In their role as forensic clinicians, psychologists conduct forensic mental health assessments of criminal offenders (in criminal cases) and civil litigants (in civil cases) in numerous legal contexts (see Heilbrun, DeMatteo, Brooks Holliday, & LaDuke, 2014; Melton et al., 2018). Unlike traditional clinical assessments (described in Chapter 1), which are conducted to develop a psychological treatment plan for individuals with mental health symptoms, forensic mental health assessments assist legal decision-makers – typically attorneys, judges, and juries – to make better-informed decisions in legal cases in which psychological expertise can be useful to the legal process. In this role, forensic psychologists are using their expertise regarding human behavior, interviewing and testing, and legal standards to educate attorneys, courts, and juries about some relationship between psychology and the law.

In a criminal context, forensic psychologists may evaluate criminal defendants to address a variety of legal questions, including:

- Competence to stand trial: The Supreme Court of the United States has interpreted the U.S. Constitution as requiring that defendants be competent before they can stand trial in court for their crime (*Dusky v. United States*, 1960). In all federal courts and most states, competence to stand trial is interpreted to mean that the defendant (a) has a sufficient understanding of his or her legal situation and (b) can offer meaningful assistance to the defense attorney. It would be

fundamentally unfair to put someone on trial, which could potentially result in the imposition of a harsh sentence, if that person was
not competent. These are the most commonly performed evaluations by forensic psychologists (Melton et al., 2018). Offenders who
are determined to be incompetent to stand trial receive treatment to
restore their competence before the legal proceedings resume. The
Supreme Court has also held that criminal defendants must be
competent to enter a guilty plea, using the same legal standard
(*Godinez* v. *Moran*, 1993).

CASE BRIEF

In *Sell* v. *United States* (2003), the United States Supreme Court ruled that
criminal defendants deemed incompetent to stand trial can only be forcibly
medicated for purposes of competency restoration under very limited
circumstances. Today, forced medication hearings for purposes of competency
restoration are commonly referred to as *Sell* hearings.

CASE BRIEF

In *Dusky* v. *United States* (1960), the United States Supreme Court established the
minimum standard for determining whether a criminal defendant is competent to
stand trial. To be capable of standing trial, criminal defendants must have
a factual and rational understanding of the case against them and possess
a sufficient ability to assist their attorney in the defense.

CASE BRIEF

In *Jackson* v. *Indiana* (1972), the United States Supreme Court ruled it
unconstitutional to indefinitely commit a criminal defendant deemed incompetent
to stand trial. Rather, a criminal defendant can only remain committed if there is
a possibility the defendant may be restored to competency in the foreseeable
future.

- Competence to waive Miranda rights: As most viewers of crime television shows know, people suspected of committing a crime cannot be interrogated by the police unless they are first read their Miranda rights. A typical Miranda warning notifies suspects that they have the right to remain silent, anything they say can and will be used against them in a court of law, and they have the right to have an attorney present during the interrogation (*Miranda* v. *Arizona*, 1966). If a suspect waives these Miranda rights, he or she can be interrogated by the police, who are ultimately trying to obtain a confession from the suspect. A legal issue that comes up in some of these contexts is whether the suspect was competent to waive his or her Miranda rights, particularly if the resulting interrogation led to a confession. Forensic psychologists who conduct evaluations of competence to waive Miranda rights focus on whether the suspect understood the rights as presented by the police and whether the suspect knowingly, intelligently, and voluntarily waived those rights before being interrogated. If the results of an evaluation reveal that the suspect did not understand the Miranda rights or waive them appropriately, the confession that resulted from the police interrogation cannot be used by the prosecution.
- Competence to be executed: A criminal offender who has been sentenced to death can only be executed if he or she is competent to be executed. In *Ford* v. *Wainwright* (1986) and *Panetti* v. *Quarterman* (2007), the Supreme Court of the United States held that an offender is competent to be executed if the offender is aware execution is imminent and understands why he or she is being executed. These types of evaluations are relatively rare because the number of executions in the United States has declined in recent years, but they are conducted when there is some concern that an inmate on death row lacks the competence to be executed.

FORENSIC FUN FACT

A commonly used insanity defense test in the United States, the M'Naghten Rule, has its origins in British common law. In 1843, Daniel M'Naghten was acquitted of murder charges after intending to assassinate British Prime Minister Robert Peel, but mistakenly shooting his private secretary, Edward Drummond. M'Naghten – who had paranoid delusions – was acquitted after he was deemed to have been suffering from mental illness that made him unable to appreciate his actions and/ or appreciate that his actions were wrong.

- Insanity: Insanity is a criminal defense in which the defendant argues that he or she should not be held legally responsible for a crime due to a mental health problem. Whereas evaluations of criminal competencies, including competence to stand trial, competence to waive Miranda rights, and competence to be executed, focus on the offender's present mental health functioning, insanity evaluations focus on the defendant's mental health functioning at the time the offense was committed. Although there are several insanity tests used across states, they typically require that the offender was experiencing a significant mental health problem at the time of the offense that resulted in the offender's inability to recognize criminal actions as wrong or to control such actions. If an offender is found not guilty by reason of insanity (or NGRI), the offender is committed to a secure psychiatric facility to receive treatment and will only be released when he or she is no longer a risk to public safety. The attempted assassination of President Reagan by John Hinckley, Jr., is a well-known insanity case. Hinckley was found NGRI due to the presence of severe mental illness at the time he shot President Reagan. One final point. As may be clear, insanity is a legal construct, not a mental health diagnosis, so a defendant can be found NGRI, but not diagnosed as insane.

DID YOU KNOW?

Although the insanity defense receives a lot of popular attention, it is used very rarely – in approximately 1% of criminal cases. Further, when a defendant pleads NGRI, the defense is only successful in approximately 25% of those cases.

- Juvenile waiver: In every state, there are situations in which an adolescent who commits a crime can be tried in court as an adult (NeMoyer, 2018). This usually applies when adolescents are accused of serious crimes, such as murder, aggravated assault, kidnapping, or certain sexual offenses, because of society's interest in punishing these types of serious offenses. Typically, adolescent offenders have their cases heard in juvenile/family court, but those cases are waived to criminal court if the offense is sufficiently serious. The determination of whether an adolescent offender should be adjudicated in juvenile/family court or criminal court is quite important for both the offender and society. If an adolescent's case is adjudicated in juvenile/family court, the court only has jurisdiction over the offender until he or she turns age 18 or 21 (depending on the state). If, however, the adolescent's case is heard in criminal court, the adolescent can potentially be sentenced to life in prison (depending on the severity of the crime). In juvenile waiver contexts, forensic psychologists assess the adolescent's maturity, treatment needs, and risk to public safety to help courts decide whether to hear the adolescent's case in juvenile/family court or criminal court (see Heilbrun, DeMatteo, King, & Filone, 2017).

CASE BRIEF

In *Kent* v. *United States* (1966), the United States Supreme Court held that juvenile defendants are entitled to due process rights when a court is deciding whether to transfer cases from juvenile court to criminal (adult) court. The Court did not specify a strict standard, but suggested that the following factors be considered in determining if a juvenile should be tried in criminal court: (1) seriousness of the offense charged; (2) if the offense was violent and/or premeditated; (3) victim of the offense (person or property); (4) whether the case had prosecutorial merit; (5) if the juvenile had adult co-defendants; (6) sophistication and maturity of the juvenile; (7) juvenile's offense history; and (8) the juvenile's prospects for rehabilitation and the need to protect the community from harm.

FORENSIC FUN FACT AND CASE BRIEFS

In recent years, the United States Supreme Court has greatly restricted the use of the justice system's harshest punishments for juvenile offenders. In *Roper* v. *Simmons* (2005), the Supreme Court held that it was unconstitutional to sentence a juvenile defendant to death. In *Miller* v. *Alabama* (2012), the Court held that it was unconstitutional to sentence a juvenile defendant to a mandatory sentence of life without the possibility of parole. A key contributor in this shift has been psychological research indicating that adolescent brains differ substantially from adult brains.

- Conditional release: In many states, offenders serving a prison sentence can be released early on parole. Sometimes inmates are released due to "good behavior" and other times they are released due to prison overcrowding. Before a prisoner is released on parole, a state parole board may ask for an evaluation of the likelihood that the prisoner will commit another crime if released. These evaluations for parole suitability are often performed by forensic psychologists.

DID YOU KNOW?

When forensic psychologists assess risk for antisocial behavior, they may not just focus on *predicting* risk – they may also focus on *managing* or *reducing/mitigating* risk. In those cases, the forensic report may discuss factors that contribute to increased risk for negative behavior and factors (or interventions) that may decrease risk.

CASE BRIEF

In *Barefoot* v. *Estelle* (1983), the United States Supreme Court ruled that it was acceptable for mental health experts to offer opinions about a criminal defendant's risk for future danger.

- State/federal sentencing: Forensic psychologists may conduct evaluations to help state and federal courts determine appropriate sentences for defendants who have been convicted of a crime. In most states, an offender's mental health functioning and any risk the offender poses to the public are considered by courts when determining an appropriate sentence, and forensic psychologists are well suited to examine these and other factors that play an important role in sentencing contexts.

CASE BRIEF

In *Atkins* v. *Virginia* (2002), the United States Supreme Court ruled that it violated the 8th Amendment's proscription against cruel and unusual punishment to sentence individuals with an intellectual disability to the death penalty.

CASE BRIEF

In *Ake* v. *Oklahoma* (1985), the United States Supreme Court held that indigent (without means) defendants in death penalty cases were entitled to a psychiatric evaluation. Though this psychiatric evaluation could be used on the defendant's behalf, it is paid for by the state.

- Capital mitigation (death penalty): After a criminal defendant is convicted of a crime for which the death penalty is a potential punishment, the court must determine whether to sentence the defendant to death or life in prison. Forensic psychologists may be called upon to help the defense argue that death is not an appropriate punishment for a particular defendant due to the presence of certain factors (called mitigating factors) that would make a death sentence too harsh. Some of these mitigating factors relate to the defendant's past or current mental health functioning. Forensic psychologists may also be called on to help the prosecution argue that death is an appropriate sentence for a particular defendant due to the presence of aggravating factors (e.g., heinous offense, history of violence, high likelihood of future violence).

EXAMPLES OF LEGAL QUESTIONS ADDRESSED BY FORENSIC PSYCHOLOGISTS IN CRIMINAL CONTEXTS

- Competence to stand trial
- Competence to waive Miranda rights
- Competence to be executed
- Insanity
- Juvenile waiver
- Conditional release
- State/federal sentencing
- Capital mitigation

The ultimate decisions in these cases are made by the court (judge or jury, depending on the case and decision being made), but forensic psychologists can help the court to better understand the offender's mental health functioning and how it relates to the legal question being addressed in the case.

In civil law contexts, forensic psychologists evaluate individuals who are involved or may become involved in litigation or some other civil proceeding. These types of evaluations can be requested by attorneys and courts, just like in criminal law contexts, but they may also be requested by employers and insurance companies. Some of the forensic mental health assessments conducted in civil contexts include:

- Civil competencies: As with criminal competencies, individuals need to be competent to engage in certain actions that fall within the civil law system. For example, people need to be competent to enter into a contract, execute a will, or make certain medical/treatment decisions. If a medical professional or family member has concerns about an individual's competence in any of these contexts, a forensic psychologist may be asked to evaluate the person's competence to help a court determine if the person can engage in these activities. In cases in which an individual is determined to lack competence, a guardian may be appointed to make these decisions on behalf of the individual.

- Disability benefits: In some contexts, employees can seek to obtain disability benefits based on their inability to perform the requirements of the job due to their mental health functioning. For example, a factory worker may claim he or she is unable to fulfill his job responsibilities due to depression, or a physician may claim he or she is not able to care for her patients due to anxiety. Forensic psychologists often assist insurance companies in determining whether these claimants should receive disability benefits by assessing the scope and extent of the claimant's mental health impairment.

- Professional malpractice: If a consumer of psychological services believes the psychologist has provided substandard professional care, the consumer can sue the psychologist for malpractice. If the lawsuit is successful, the psychologist may be required to pay monetary damages to the consumer. In these contexts, a forensic psychologist may be asked to offer an opinion about whether the psychologist's conduct fell below a minimally acceptable threshold of professional behavior.

- Psychological damages: Individuals who have been harmed can sue the person who inflicted the harm. For example, the victim of a car accident can sue the other driver for damages the victim sustained. Those damages can include physical injuries (e.g., broken bones), but also include psychological injuries (e.g., post-traumatic stress disorder, traumatic brain injury). Forensic psychologists may be asked to evaluate the scope of emotional, psychological, and cognitive harm sustained by the injured party.

- Workplace violence: In some contexts, employers who believe that an employee poses a risk of workplace violence can require the employee to undergo an evaluation by a forensic psychologist to determine whether the employee poses a heightened risk of violence. These types of evaluations are future-oriented, which means that the forensic psychologist is predicting the future likelihood that the employee will engage in violence.

CASE BRIEF

In *O'Connor* v. *Donaldson* (1975), the United States Supreme Court held that mental illness by itself was insufficient to commit a person to an institution involuntarily. Rather, there must be evidence of mental illness *and* dangerousness.

- Civil commitment: Individuals who are mentally ill and a risk of serious harm to themselves or others can be committed to a secure psychiatric facility against their will. Involuntarily hospitalizing someone who has not yet violated the law is a serious decision with significant constitutional implications, so courts want to ensure that people are not being inappropriately hospitalized if some other type of less restrictive intervention is available. Forensic psychologists often assist courts in determining if civil commitment is appropriate.

CASE BRIEF

In *Kansas* v. *Hendricks* (1997), the United States Supreme Court ruled it constitutional to civilly commit individuals who are predisposed to sexual offending and deemed unable to control their dangerousness. The Court held that because the commitment was civil – as opposed to criminal – in nature, it was not considered punishment. Therefore, it did not violate the double jeopardy or ex-post facto provisions of the U.S. Constitution.

- Sexually violent predator commitment: In about half of the states, convicted sex offenders who are about to be released from prison at the end of their sentence can instead be involuntarily civilly committed to a psychiatric facility (DeMatteo, Murphy, Galloway, & Krauss, 2015). Although some have argued that committing an offender to a psychiatric facility at the end of his or her sentence is unconstitutional because it is a second punishment for the same offense, the United States Supreme Court has upheld such laws (*Kansas* v. *Hendricks*, 1997; *United States* v. *Comstock*, 2010; see Witt & DeMatteo, 2019). For such commitments to take place, a court must determine that the offender is a sexually violent predator, and forensic psychologists may be called upon to evaluate the offender and offer an opinion of whether the offender is mentally ill and likely to engage in predatory acts of sexual violence.

EXAMPLES OF LEGAL QUESTIONS ADDRESSED BY FORENSIC PSYCHOLOGISTS IN CIVIL CONTEXTS

- Civil competencies
- Disability benefits
- Professional malpractice
- Psychological damages
- Workplace violence
- Civil commitment
- Sexually violent predator status

Family law is part of the civil law system, and forensic psychologists conduct a variety of evaluations in the family law context:

- Child custody: In the context of a divorce, parents may argue about who should have custody of the children once the parents separate. In all jurisdictions, the legal standard used by courts in child custody determinations is "the best interests of the child." Forensic psychologists are often asked to conduct child custody evaluations to help courts make these determinations.
- Child abuse and neglect: In cases of suspected child abuse or neglect, forensic psychologists may be asked to (a) help determine whether the allegations are founded and (b) assess the scope and effects of the alleged abuse. These findings can then be used to help determine if

the child should be removed from the parent's care and whether the child needs any services (e.g., therapy).

- Legal guardianship: Individuals with mental health impairments that are severe enough to substantially inhibit their ability to make independent decisions may have a guardian appointed by a court to handle their affairs. In this context, a forensic psychologist will assess whether an individual suffers from a mental health impairment that results in the person lacking the capacity to meet the essential requirements for personal healthcare, safety, therapeutic needs, financial needs, or habitation (or living situation) without the assistance of a guardian.

- Parental fitness: Forensic psychologists may be asked to assess the capacity of a parent to provide the necessary emotional, cognitive, and financial support for children. In extreme cases, parental rights can be terminated by the court, in which case the parent loses the legal rights to raise the child and make important decisions about the child's care and upbringing (e.g., which doctor to use, whether the child should be raised in a particular religion, which school the child should attend).

EXAMPLES OF LEGAL QUESTIONS ADDRESSED BY FORENSIC PSYCHOLOGISTS IN FAMILY LAW CONTEXTS

- Child custody
- Child abuse and neglect
- Parental fitness

In forensic assessment contexts, forensic psychologists are appointed by a court or hired by an attorney, insurance company, or employer to conduct an evaluation based on a legal question. Conducting a forensic mental health assessment can include a variety of components, with the scope and specifics of each evaluation based on the type of legal question being addressed. However, in a typical scenario, a forensic mental health assessment includes a comprehensive review of all available records (e.g., school, medical, mental health, employment, arrest), interviewing and psychological testing of the examinee (and sometimes other individuals involved in the case), interviewing third parties (e.g., family members, employers, teachers, therapists, probation officers), writing a report, and occasionally providing expert testimony in a deposition, hearing, trial, or administrative proceeding.

Forensic Therapy

The practice of clinical forensic psychology is not limited to conducting forensic assessments, and some forensic psychologists focus on providing mental health treatment to justice-involved individuals. Forensic psychologists often provide therapeutic services that are tailored to the issues and context of a specific legal proceeding. For example, a forensic psychologist employed in a secure forensic psychiatric hospital may provide "restorative therapy" to offenders who have been determined by a court to be incompetent to stand trial, or they may provide therapy designed to reduce the risk of violence posed by an offender who has been found NGRI. Other forensic psychologists may provide treatment to reduce the risk of recidivism posed by convicted sex offenders, or they may work with juveniles in a juvenile detention center to reduce the likelihood they will violate the law once they are released. Of note, simply conducting therapy with a criminal offender or civil litigant does not automatically make the activity "forensic," even if the therapy occurs in a correctional facility or forensic psychiatric hospital; rather, in therapy contexts, the treatment is only considered forensic if the therapy is provided to an offender or litigant in a legal context in which a legal decision-maker needs to make a decision about the offender or litigant.

Forensic Researchers

Recall that under the broad definition of forensic psychology, the practice of forensic psychology is not limited to the assessment and treatment of individuals involved with the justice system. Many forensic psychologists are partially, primarily, or exclusively focused on conducting research and disseminating findings that can be useful to legal decision-makers or to some other aspect of the judicial system. Some forensic psychologists do not have clinical training and instead have a doctoral degree in a research-based area of psychology, so they do not have the necessary qualifications to conduct forensic assessments. Other psychologists with clinical training (either forensic or non-forensic) also integrate research into their practice. Rather than evaluating an offender or litigant, forensic researchers conduct surveys, experiments, and other studies relevant to the judicial system.

With their expertise in assessment and interventions, clinical psychologists might help develop valid and reliable screening measures to assess mental health functioning or violence risk among justice-involved individuals, or they evaluate the effects of treatment programs on reducing recidivism for different types of offenders. Social psychologists, who are trained to understand the impact of social influences on individual behavior, might study jury decision-making, jury selection, gang violence, and racial discrimination. Cognitive psychologists, who are broadly trained in human thinking, reasoning, sensation and perception, and memory, might study eyewitness identification, false confessions, investigative interviewing, deception detection, and memory accuracy. Finally, developmental psychologists, who are trained in human development across the lifespan, might study the development of psychopathic characteristics, the reliability of courtroom testimony provided by children, decision-making among children and adolescents, and the effects of divorce on children. These topic areas are not exhaustive, and there are many other topics forensic psychologists can address through research. Aside from conducting research, research-focused psychologists can consult with attorneys and courts and offer expert testimony in legal proceedings or to lawmakers and policymakers.

Forensic Consultants

There are also numerous opportunities for properly trained psychologists to engage in consultation that addresses some aspect of the judicial system. Forensic consultation can involve wide-ranging areas of expertise (e.g., clinical psychology, neuropsychology, developmental psychology) in various contexts. For example, psychologists can consult with attorneys regarding jury selection, which is the process of eliminating potential jurors who are predicted to render a verdict that would be unfavorable to the attorney's client. Psychologists may also be retained by attorneys to assist in critiquing a psychological report submitted by the opposing party's forensic expert and developing cross-examination questions that can be used to highlight weaknesses in the opposing expert's evaluation and report.

In a correctional context, forensic psychologists may be asked to recommend an efficient, valid, and reliable screening procedure to classify incoming inmates based on their mental health needs, suicide risk, or potential for violence to others. Psychologists may be also asked to provide recommendations regarding ways to improve the staffing and administrative structure of a correctional facility (which requires expertise in the specialty area of industrial/organizational psychology), offer advice on the pros and cons of segregating inmates based on crime type, discuss the negative psychological effects of solitary confinement, or train correctional officers on de-escalation strategies they can use when confronted with a volatile inmate. Alternatively, consultation in a correctional context may be focused on assisting the facility to provide evidence-based psychological treatment to improve the mental health functioning of inmates.

Consultation with police departments is becoming increasingly popular as law enforcement agencies recognize the valuable contributions psychologists can make to the field (Bartol & Bartol, 2018). When working with police departments, psychologists may be asked to develop screening procedures for selecting the best candidates for the police academy or to determine the ideal shift schedules for police officers. Forensic psychologists may also assist police departments in developing mental health assessment and treatment protocols for officers involved in shootings. In recent years, forensic psychologists have been influential in training police officers and other first responders (e.g., Emergency Medical Technicians) to interact more effectively with individuals who are mentally ill and/or drug-involved. Such training has resulted in healthier police–citizen interactions and fewer injuries to police officers and citizens.

Psychologists may also be asked to consult with schools, courts, government agencies, and legislative bodies. In response to several highly tragic school shootings, psychologists are being asked to collaborate with schools and law enforcement agencies to develop effective "active-shooter" safety protocols.

In recent years, numerous courts in the United States have developed specialty dockets to address the specific needs of offenders with behavioral health disorders. For example, drug courts were developed to address the needs of non-violent drug offenders, while mental health courts were developed to handle cases involving offenders with mental health disorders. Psychologists can help courts to develop, implement, monitor, and analyze these programs. Psychologists may be asked by government agencies that focus on the well-being of children (e.g., Children and Youth; Department of Children and Families) to review organizational policies related to handling child abuse and neglect cases, including how children can be interviewed by law enforcement – without causing additional trauma to the children – during the course of an investigation. Finally, psychologists may be asked to testify before legislative or administrative bodies to summarize research in a particular area or discuss ways in which certain laws or policies can be developed or modified based on psychological research.

Employment Settings

In conducting the activities described above, forensic psychologists can work in a variety of settings. Some forensic psychologists are based in traditional academic settings, such as a college or university, where they teach courses, conduct research, publish articles and books, and provide forensic psychological services. Forensic psychologists can also be found in private practice, child protection agencies, government agencies, courts, psychiatric hospitals, correctional facilities, juvenile detention centers, research organizations, law enforcement agencies, and legal advocacy centers, among many other settings. For some psychologists, forensic psychology is their primary job, while others integrate forensic psychology into a wider variety of professional activities. Jobs and employment settings for forensic psychologists are discussed in detail in Chapter 10.

★ ★ ★

CONCLUSION

Although the relationship between psychology and law dates back many hundreds of years, forensic psychology as a stand-alone profession is relatively new. Several key events in the early to mid 20th century sparked interest in forensic psychology, and the field has experienced rapid growth in the past few decades. The range and type of activities performed by forensic psychologists, which encompass assessments, treatment, research, and consultation, are continuing to expand as forensic psychologists become even more integrated – and essential – to the justice system. Now that we have defined forensic psychology, briefly described its history, and discussed the current activities of forensic psychologists, we can turn our attention to discussing how those interested in pursuing a career in forensic psychology can become competitive for admission to graduate training programs, which is the focus of Chapter 3.

REFERENCES

Ake v. Oklahoma, 470 U.S. 68 (1985).
Atkins v. Virginia, 536 U.S. 304 (2002).
Barefoot v. Estelle, 463 U.S. 880 (1983).
Bartol, C. R., & Bartol, A. M. (2018). *Introduction to forensic psychology: Research and application* (5th ed.). Thousand Oaks, CA: SAGE Publications.
Brown v. Board of Education, 347 U.S. 483 (1954).
Burl, J., Shah, S., Filone, S., Foster, E., & DeMatteo, D. (2012). A survey of graduate training programs and coursework in forensic psychology. *Teaching of Psychology, 39*, 48–53.
DeMatteo, D., Marczyk, G., Krauss, D. A., & Burl, J. (2009). Educational and training models in forensic psychology. *Training and Education in Professional Psychology, 3*, 184–191.

DeMatteo, D., Murphy, M., Galloway, M., & Krauss, D. A. (2015). A national survey of United States sexually violent person legislation: Policy, procedures, and practice. *International Journal of Forensic Mental Health, 14*, 245–266.

Dusky v. United States, 362 U.S. 402 (1960).

Ford v. Wainwright, 477 U.S. 399 (1986).

Godinez v. Moran, 509 U.S. 389 (1993).

Grisso, T., & Brodsky, S. L. (Eds.). (2018). *The roots of modern psychology and law: A narrative history.* New York: Oxford University Press.

Heilbrun, K., DeMatteo, D., Brooks Holliday, S., & LaDuke, C. (Eds.). (2014). *Forensic mental health assessment: A casebook* (2nd ed.). New York: Oxford University Press.

Heilbrun, K., DeMatteo, D., King, C., & Filone, S. (2017). *Evaluating juvenile transfer and disposition: Law, science, and practice.* New York: Routledge/Taylor & Francis Group.

Jackson v. Indiana, 406 U.S. 715 (1972).

Jenkins v. United States, 307 F.2d 637 (D.C. Cir. 1962).

Kansas v. Hendricks, 521 U.S. 346 (1997).

Kent v. United States, 383 U.S. 541 (1966).

King James Bible, Gospel of Luke 23: 24.

Melton, G. B., Petrila, J., Poythress, N. G., Slobogin, C., Otto, R. K., Mossman, D., & Condie, L. O. (2018). *Psychological evaluations for the courts* (4th ed.). New York: Guilford.

Miller v. Alabama, 567 U.S. 460 (2012).

Miranda v. Arizona, 384 U.S. 486 (1966).

Munsterberg, H. (1908). *On the witness stand: Essays on psychology and crime.* New York: Doubleday.

Neal, T. M. S. (2017). Identifying the forensic psychologist role. In G. Pirelli, R. Beattey, & P. Zapf (Eds.), *The ethical practice of forensic psychology: A casebook* (pp. 1–17). Hoboken, NJ: Wiley.

NeMoyer, A. (2018). Kent revisited: Aligning judicial waiver criteria with more than fifty years of social science research. *Vermont Law Review, 42*, 441–528.

O'Connor v. Donaldson, 422 U.S. 563 (1975).

Panetti v. Quarterman, 551 U.S. 930 (2007).

Roper v. Simmons, 543 U.S. 551 (2005).

Sell v. United States, 539 U.S. 166 (2003).

United States v. Comstock, 560 U.S. 126 (2010).

Witt, P. H., & DeMatteo, D. (2019). Sexually violent predator laws: Historical development and evolution. In W. T. Donohue & D. S. Bromberg (Eds.), *Sexually violent predators: A clinical science handbook* (pp. 9–20). New York: Springer Publishing Co.

FURTHER READING

Costanzo, M., & Krauss, D. (2018). *Forensic and legal psychology: Psychological science applied to law* (3rd ed.). New York: Worth Publishers.

Ewing, C. P. (2008). *Trials of a forensic psychologist: A casebook.* Hoboken, NJ: John Wiley & Sons.

Huss, M. T. (2014). *Forensic psychology: Research, clinical practice, and applications* (2nd ed.). Hoboken, NJ: John Wiley & Sons.

Otto, R. K., & Heilbrun, K. (2002). The practice of forensic psychology: A look toward the future in light of the past. *American Psychologist, 57,* 5–18.

Roesch, R., Zapf, P. A., & Hart, S. D. (2010). *Forensic psychology and law.* Hoboken, NJ: John Wiley & Sons.

CHAPTER 3

Laying the Groundwork

Things to Know in Advance of Graduate School

Imagine you are planning to build your future dream home from the ground up. The project will be demanding, lengthy, and, eventually rewarding. Maybe you have a sense of what you would like the house to look like, but you are unsure of how to bring that vision to life. This is common. It is important to identify the first steps necessary to lay the groundwork, but with a variety of information and options in front of you, even the initial steps can be hard to navigate. The preparation phase involves identifying and obtaining the necessary tools, knowing how best to use the tools at your disposal, and creating a blueprint.

Similarly, to establish a career as a forensic psychologist, you must first develop your toolkit and build a strong foundation to pursue further training and specialization. This can be accomplished during your undergraduate or post-college years as you prepare for graduate school. The graduate school application process is challenging and competitive, and it may engender a sense of unease. The good news is you can begin laying the groundwork in advance by checking off universal requirements at the undergraduate level. You can further strengthen your chances by pursuing certain research and clinical opportunities that will give you an advantage when it comes time to apply for graduate admission.

Although there are many advantages to beginning the process of becoming a forensic psychologist early in your training, all hope is not lost if you decide on the field of forensic psychology later in life. As we discuss, you can enter the forensic field at various points in your education and training. Therefore, even if your desired career path has changed over time, familiarizing yourself with the processes involved in becoming specialized in forensic psychology

UNIVERSAL REQUIREMENTS

- ☑ Bachelor's degree (BA/BS)
- ☑ Relevant coursework for graduate program admission
- ☑ Standardized tests (Graduate Record Examinations [GRE])

STRENGTHENING YOUR CHANCES

- ☐ Additional relevant coursework
- ☐ Competitive grade point average (GPA) and standardized test scores
- ☐ Research experience
- ☐ Clinical experience

will equip you with the knowledge necessary to make choices that can improve your chances of success and fill any gaps in your existing foundation.

PREREQUISITES: DEVELOPING YOUR TOOLKIT

Bachelor's Degree and Undergraduate Coursework

Pursuing your bachelor's degree in college provides a good opportunity to check off prerequisites for graduate school applications. Many colleges offer a Bachelor of Arts (BA) or Bachelor of Science (BS) degree in psychology. Both provide adequate foundation in psychology, but the degrees often differ with regard to additional course requirements. A BA degree typically operates under a liberal arts framework, meaning additional coursework may span many disciplines including humanities (e.g., foreign language), creative arts (e.g., theater), social sciences (e.g., economics), and science (e.g., biology). In contrast, a BS degree focuses primarily on science and math and thus may involve more research- or laboratory-centered courses. Although a bachelor's degree in psychology is most common, other routes are available. Some schools offer degrees in related social science disciplines (e.g., human development), or you could major in another subject and complete a minor in psychology or a related discipline.

Regardless of the undergraduate degree you earn, the key is to complete relevant coursework for admission into graduate programs in psychology. Although there are typically no set prerequisites across programs, applicants may benefit from a carefully selected variety of psychology courses. Core coursework often consists of introductory psychology courses and foundational topics, including social, developmental, cognitive, and abnormal psychology. Additionally, core courses may include research-related topics, such as research methods and statistics (Norcross, Sayette, Stratigis, & Zimmerman, 2014). To set yourself apart, you could also choose to enroll in specialized courses, including ones that focus on psychological assessment or the psychology of personality, both of which are relevant to forensic psychology.

Although not required, it is advantageous to complete additional coursework directly related to forensic psychology. The number of undergraduate forensic psychology courses is increasing, and many colleges and universities are offering at least one course in forensic psychology (Burl, Shah, Filone, Foster, & DeMatteo, 2012; DeMatteo, Marczyk, Krauss, & Burl, 2009). Some of the more commonly offered undergraduate courses include forensic psychology, the psychology of juries, and survey courses that focus broadly on law–psychology topics. A more recent development is the offering of undergraduate degrees in forensic psychology. For example, John Jay College of Criminal Justice currently offers a BA in Forensic Psychology that provides training in psychological theory, research methods, and the application of psychological principles to specific areas in the legal system.

In addition to taking foundational psychology courses, it is beneficial to demonstrate a strong pattern of academic achievement as reflected by your grade point average (GPA). Graduate programs differ with regard to minimum academic achievement requirements, but a common cutoff is a 3.2 GPA, with average GPA scores hovering around 3.5 (Pagano, Wicherski, & Kohout, 2010). Of note, master's programs tend to be less competitive than doctoral programs, so doctoral programs typically prefer a higher GPA. Some graduate programs may ask applicants to report two GPAs: overall average performance across all undergraduate coursework and average performance across all psychology courses. Both GPAs impact admission decisions, but greater emphasis may be placed on the psychology-specific GPA, depending on the program. Additional indicators of academic achievement that may improve chances of gaining admission to graduate school include academic awards (e.g., scholarships, academic honors, performance awards for classes or academic competitions) and induction into an academic honor society, such as Psi Chi (an international honor society in psychology).

Standardized Tests

Many U.S.-based graduate programs in psychology require applicants to take the Graduate Record Examinations (GRE) General Test, which is a standardized test consisting of written, multiple-choice, and numeric entry questions that assess three domains: Verbal Reasoning, Quantitative Reasoning, and Analytical Writing. Per the latest version (2011) of the GRE, Verbal Reasoning and Quantitative Reasoning scores range from 130 to

170, and Analytical Writing scores range from 0 to 6. Gaining acceptance to graduate school is based in part on an applicant's GRE scores. A survey of admissions data conducted by the American Psychological Association during the 2008–09 academic year examined average GRE score requirements for master's and doctoral programs (Pagano et al., 2010) (Table 3.1). In general, GRE scores were lower for master's programs than for doctoral programs, but keep in mind that similar to GPA scores, minimum and average GRE scores differ by school and degree.

Additionally, some programs recommend or require the GRE Psychology Test, which is a subject test consisting of multiple-choice questions drawn from various areas of psychology, including biological, cognitive, social, developmental, clinical, and measurement/methodology. Some programs will require the subject test only for applicants who did not major in psychology as an undergraduate. Regardless of program requirements, if you did not complete an undergraduate degree in psychology, the GRE Psychology Test presents an opportunity for you to demonstrate to admissions committees your proficiency and interest in the field.

You may feel nervous at the prospect of having a bad test day or of your ability to obtain a competitive test score. Educational Testing Service (ETS), the organization that develops and administers the GRE, allows test takers to re-take the exam once every 21 days, with a maximum of five attempts during a 12-month period. Furthermore, the ScoreSelect option allows test-takers to choose which scores they wish to report to graduate programs, enabling applicants to put their best foot forward. Nonetheless, advanced preparation is important to ensure that you have enough time to master the content and flexibility to report optimal scores to graduate programs. Free test preparation materials, including sample questions and test structure, are available on the ETS website. Additionally, a variety of books published by both ETS and other test prep

Table 3.1 Minimum and Average Graduate Record Examinations (GRE) Scores by Type of Degree[1]

		Master's	Doctoral
Minimum GRE Score	Verbal	152	154
	Quantitative	144	145
	Total	296	299
Median GRE Score	Verbal	154	158
	Quantitative	148	151
	Total	304	309

companies (e.g., Princeton Review, Magoosh) and prep courses are available to help you maximize your performance on test day. GRE scores remain valid and reportable for 5 years from the test date for exams completed on or after July 1, 2016 (ETS, n.d.).

In sum, a bachelor's degree, GPA, and GRE scores are all required to apply to graduate school, and you can improve your chances of admission by completing relevant coursework. However, there is considerable variability in terms of expectations and minimum standards across graduate programs. Graduate schools typically provide information regarding mandatory or preferred minimums for GPA and GRE scores and admissions data for incoming classes on their program websites.

RECOMMENDATIONS: MAXIMIZING THE TOOLS AT YOUR DISPOSAL

There are several other ways to strengthen your application for graduate school. Getting accepted to graduate school is a competitive process, but you can improve your chances of admission by seeking out research and clinical opportunities both during and after your undergraduate training. It is also worth keeping in mind that the time prior to graduate school is just as important for exploring different options and determining what you are passionate about as it is for building an impressive curriculum vitae (CV).

A **curriculum vitae (CV)** is similar in content and function to a resume, with minor differences. Both present a summary of an applicant's background, skills, and expertise. However, CVs are generally lengthier and are intended to showcase academic accomplishments and educational background. They are typically requested in academic contexts, whereas resumes are more appropriate for industry-related job markets (Hull Strategies, 2016).

Research Experience

Conducting research is typically an important component of graduate training in psychology, so gaining research experience will help to distinguish you during the application process. Research experience may take many forms, including volunteering in a research lab, completing an honors or senior thesis in college, or working full-time as a research assistant. Although helpful, it is not necessary to match your prior research experience with the specific program to which you ultimately apply. There is significant value to familiarizing yourself with the research process in general and to determining the type of research that best suits you. Furthermore, research involvement can be useful for networking and building professional skills through attending professional conferences, creating presentations, or co-authoring manuscripts.

Clinical Experience

Gaining experience working with clinical populations and offenders is another strategy to strengthen yourself as a candidate for graduate school admission. Although few clinical job opportunities are available to those without advanced degrees, volunteer positions are more readily accessible. For example, experiences with university-based peer mental health services, crisis hotlines, or educational programs in correctional facilities provide on-the-ground training that fosters the development of clinical skills.

In addition to a strong academic background and standardized test scores, obtaining research or clinical experience will not only set you apart as a graduate applicant, but also prepare you for many of the responsibilities you will be performing in graduate school. Having forensically relevant experiences is ideal, but gaining familiarity with research and clinical work is most important. There are also opportunities that provide both research and clinical experience, such as clinical trials, which is a type of research that involves the investigation of clinical interventions. These experiences will boost your resume and/or CV and build a network of individuals who can attest to your capabilities within the field.

GRADUATE PROGRAMS AND DEGREES: CREATING A BLUEPRINT

Although the prerequisites and opportunities previously discussed are common tools to prepare you for most graduate schools, much of the necessary preparation will depend on the type of graduate program or degree you wish to pursue. Your degree of choice in turn has implications for your career. Deciding which type of degree is best for you is not easy because it involves several considerations, such as program length, the availability of financial support, and the type of training received. Once you have settled on a type of degree, another set of considerations becomes relevant, including the program's research faculty, accreditation status of the program, and relative focus on research versus clinical work. These factors are discussed in more detail in Chapter 4; for now, we will introduce the various degrees that are available.

Doctoral Degrees	Master's Degrees
PhD	MS/MA
PsyD	MSW
DSW	
MD/DO	
	Joint Degrees
	JD/PhD
	JD/PsyD
	JD/MS (or MA)

Doctoral Degrees

Obtaining a doctoral degree in clinical psychology with a specialization in forensic psychology is a common route to becoming a forensic psychologist. Non-clinical, research-based doctoral degrees in related areas (e.g., experimental psychology) are also available. Doctoral degrees provide intensive and thorough academic, clinical, and research training, and they afford the greatest latitude in terms of career options. Doctoral programs are lengthy and consist of many requirements, including coursework and completion of a dissertation. Some doctoral programs also involve completion of a thesis project and master's degree along the way. Clinical doctoral degrees are a particular subset that are intended for those who wish to provide clinical services, such as therapy or mental health evaluations, in addition to conducting research. In addition to the model described above, these degrees provide intensive clinical training and the potential for obtaining licensure as a psychologist. In most states, a clinical doctoral degree is required to pursue licensure as a psychologist. Additional components include clinical practicum (i.e., field experience whereby graduate students receive supervised training as clinicians) and a 1-year internship.

Master's Degrees

Master's degrees can be useful building blocks along the way to applying to doctoral programs. Master's programs often consist of psychology coursework and completion of a thesis project. Depending on the program, you may also gain additional research and perhaps clinical experience. At this level, a wider variety of related areas of study are available, including clinical or counseling psychology, forensic psychology, and criminal justice. Although your ability to become licensed with a master's degree is more limited, completion of this degree may strengthen your position as a candidate for doctoral programs or equip you for jobs in research settings.

Other Degrees

A few alternative routes to a career in forensic psychology are worth noting. Those with clinical social work degrees, including a Master of Social Work (MSW) or Doctor of Social Work (DSW), may pursue licensure as a clinical social worker (LCSW) after completing additional hours of direct social work experience; they can then pursue certification in forensic social work either through an accredited university or a national forensic association (e.g., National Association of Certified Child Forensic Interviewers) (Psychology School Guide, n.d.). Alternatively, those with a Doctor of Medicine (MD) or Doctor of Osteopathy (DO) degree with a specialization in psychiatry can seek opportunities to complete a forensic rotation, residency, or fellowship. Finally, some graduate schools offer joint-degree programs that are relevant to forensic psychology. For example, students in law–psychology programs may simultaneously obtain Juris Doctor (JD; a law degree)[2] and PhD or master's degrees.

GRADUATE SCHOOL AND BEYOND: LAYING THE GROUNDWORK THROUGH SPECIALIZATION

Similar to the options available to pursue academic, research, and clinical opportunities, there are many roads to specialization and training in forensic psychology. You may follow a direct path from a doctoral program with a forensic track through postdoctoral fellowship, with forensic research and clinical training along the way. Alternatively, you may choose to mix and match. Although there is no "right way," keep in mind that the greater and more varied your experiences are within the field of forensic psychology, the better you are setting yourself up for future success in the field.

Doctoral Programs: Forensic Major Area of Study

As previously mentioned, a doctoral degree in psychology is typically required to pursue a career as a forensic psychologist. However, the specifics of this approach can look different depending on the individual and program. Although the bulk of specialization occurs after graduate school, many doctoral programs will have tracks or major areas of study for a subfield within psychology. Common tracks include child psychology, neuropsychology, and health psychology. Although less common, some programs offer forensic tracks, and other doctoral programs have a full forensic focus. These will be discussed at greater length in Chapter 4.

A **track, or major area of study**, concentrates on a subfield of psychology (e.g., neuropsychology). It directs students' research, clinical training, and academic focus beyond the more general clinical psychology training.

Clinical Experience: Forensic Practicum and Internship

What happens if you wind up at a doctoral program without a forensic track? Now what? This may require you to become more of a self-starter, but you can still pursue forensic training opportunities. One option is through your clinical placements. In a doctoral program, clinical training comes in the form of two primary experiences: clinical practicum and predoctoral internship. Practicum experiences, which typically begin in the first or second year of a doctoral program, are clinical training opportunities that provide supervision by a licensed clinician and firsthand experience providing clinical services (e.g., psychotherapy, psychological testing). Doctoral students typically transition through multiple practicum placements throughout their training. These practicum placements build up to the capstone clinical training experience: predoctoral internship. A predoctoral internship is a 1-year full-time clinical placement that provides supervised experiences that are required for licensure as a psychologist.

Depending on the geographic location of your program, it may be possible to obtain forensic experience through a practicum placement. Some examples include forensic assessment and treatment centers, inpatient forensic psychiatric units, and correctional facilities. You may also

Practicum
Clinical training opportunity – involving supervision and firsthand experience providing clinical services – that occurs during graduate school

Predoctoral Internship
One-year full-time clinical placement, involving supervised clinical experiences, that occurs prior to receiving a doctorate degree

Fellowship
Postdoctoral training – involving research, clinical work, or a combination of both – that occurs after receiving a doctorate degree

seek out training through a doctoral internship with a major or minor forensic focus. Keep in mind, however, that the internship process is competitive (as discussed in Chapter 7), and it is challenging to secure a full forensic internship without prior forensic experience.

Fellowship: Postdoctoral Training

Postdoctoral training presents an additional opportunity for forensic specialization after completing an internship and receiving your doctoral degree. Securing a postdoctoral fellowship, commonly referred to as a "postdoc," enables you to gain supervised clinical hours required for licensure as a psychologist. Postdocs may be research-focused, clinical-focused, or some combination of both, and they may also involve teaching. Although specialization at the postdoc level can be a promising route to a career as a forensic psychologist, it is not necessary to complete a formal postdoctoral experience. The key consideration is obtaining sufficient supervised experience in the field, which can be obtained through a formal postdoc or through on-the-job training/supervision.

★ ★ ★

CONCLUSION

Hopefully by now you feel more familiar with what it takes to become a forensic psychologist. You may also feel more confused than ever! Although there are traditional blueprints for becoming a forensic psychologist, there are several alternative routes. Your specific blueprint will ultimately depend on your experience, goals, interests, and available opportunities.

The process of building a career as a forensic psychologist is long and effortful, so equipping yourself with the tools necessary to succeed and set yourself apart is important. Knowing what lies ahead in terms of different options for graduate school and specialization can help direct your decisions early on. That being said, throughout this chapter, you may have felt anxious because you did not have it all figured out. Worry not! The foundational information presented in this chapter provides insight into your options based on decisions you have already made. The remaining chapters will discuss each of the stages from graduate school onward and will offer tips to help you determine what makes the most sense for you.

NOTES

1 Scores reported in Pagano et al. (2010) have been converted to the scoring scale of the latest version (2011) of the GRE.
2 To apply to a JD program, it is necessary to take the Law School Admission Test, a standardized test consisting of a writing sample and multiple-choice questions assessing reading comprehension, analytical reasoning, and logical reasoning. Additional information can be found on the Law School Admission Council website: www.lsac.org.

REFERENCES

Burl, J., Shah, S., Filone, S., Foster, E., & DeMatteo, D. (2012). A survey of graduate training programs and coursework in forensic psychology. *Teaching of Psychology, 39*, 48–53.

DeMatteo, D., Marczyk, G., Krauss, D. A., & Burl, J. (2009). Educational and training models in forensic psychology. *Training and Education in Professional Psychology, 3*, 184–191.

ETS. (n.d.). *Frequently asked questions about the GRE® General Test.* Retrieved on July 19, 2019 from www.ets.org/gre/revised_general/faq/

Hull Strategies. (2016). *Some differences between résumés and CVs.* Retrieved on July 19, 2019 from www.apa.org/careers/resources/job-seekers/differences-resumes.aspx

Norcross, J. C., Sayette, M. A., Stratigis, K. Y., & Zimmerman, B. E. (2014). Of course: Prerequisite courses for admission into APA-accredited clinical and counseling psychology programs. *Society for the Teaching of Psychology, 41*, 360–364.

Pagano, V., Wicherski, M., & Kohout, J. (2010). *2010 graduate study in psychology: Test scores and requirements for Master's and Doctoral students in U.S. and Canadian graduate departments of psychology: 2008-2009.* Washington, DC: American Psychological Association.

Psychology School Guide. (n.d.). *Forensic social worker careers.* Retrieved on July 19, 2019 from www.psychologyschoolguide.net/social-work-careers/forensic-social-worker-careers/

Part II

Graduate Training

CHAPTER 4

The Paradox of Choice

Picking the Right Program

Perhaps the most pressing question facing any future forensic psychologist is, "What type of degree should I get?" After all, the type of training received in graduate school is directly related to the future career opportunities open to a forensic psychologist – higher levels of training and credentialing yield a greater breadth of potential career directions and opportunities. As discussed in Chapter 1, forensic psychology can be broadly defined as including any overlap between psychology and the legal system. As such, career opportunities are expansive, and picking the right training path to successfully target the areas of forensic psychology that an individual is most attracted to is essential. This chapter focuses on helping you to assess the various training paths that currently exist by examining the pros and cons of each approach. Doing so will allow you to make an informed decision before investing a lot of time (and potentially a lot of money!) into pursuing your chosen training path.

TYPES OF TRAINING PROGRAMS

As noted in Chapter 3, there are several graduate degree options for those interested in becoming a forensic psychologist. These include degrees in clinical psychology, such as Master of Arts (MA), Master of Science (MS), Doctor of Psychology (PsyD), Doctor of Philosophy (PhD), and joint degrees in which students pursue one of the aforementioned degrees in conjunction with a Juris Doctor (JD) or Master of Legal Studies (MLS) degree. Further, there are several types of non-clinical psychology degree programs, such as a PhD in social psychology, PhD in criminology, PhD in counseling psychology, or Doctor of Education (EdD).

Master's Degrees

Master's degrees typically provide students with a foundation in some subfield of psychology (e.g., clinical, forensic, experimental). Master's programs in psychology are often heavily focused on coursework, surveying a range of topics including research design, statistics, and foundational subfields of psychology (e.g., developmental, cognitive, social). Many master's programs also offer elective courses, which allows students to pursue topics of specific interest to them (e.g., health psychology, personality assessment). Due to their shorter duration (typically 2–3 years), master's programs may not focus on direct client contact – also known as *clinical work* – to the extent that doctoral programs do. Although some master's programs include clinical components, clinical work is not a requirement across all programs and, if provided, it may be less rigorous than the clinical expectations of doctoral-level students.

Master's degrees come in two forms: MA and MS. As previously noted, both degrees are focused on giving students a generalized survey of subject matter pertinent to psychology. However, they typically differ in terms of the focus on student-driven research. Although both types of master's programs may allow students to become involved in research, MS programs typically require students to complete an independent research project. This project often involves designing and conducting a research study, drafting a comprehensive paper, and defending the research study in front of a committee of faculty members. In contrast, MA programs may not have a requirement for an empirical research project, although they may require some other specialized project to be completed before the degree can be earned.

Unlike a doctoral degree, a master's degree may be either a terminal degree (meaning that the graduate program is completed upon receipt of the degree) or earned as an intermediate step towards a doctoral degree (meaning that the student is enrolled in a doctoral program and earns a master's degree along the way to the doctoral degree). Whether the master's degree is earned as an intermediate step or is earned as a terminal degree can have a significant impact on educational costs. As many doctoral programs provide tuition remission (i.e., no or low tuition in exchange for fulfilling teaching and other obligations), those who earn a master's degree while enrolled in a doctoral program often do so at little to no cost. In contrast, those earning a master's degree as a terminal degree are usually beholden to whatever financial aid package the program may offer and may even have to foot the whole bill!

Clinical Psychology Doctoral Degrees

A master's degree is usually not sufficient to become a licensed psychologist, though some states (e.g., Vermont, West Virginia) allow master's-level clinicians to pursue licensure upon completion of a set number of supervised clinical hours. Rather, the "norm for independent professional practice" as a researcher, clinician, or both is the doctoral degree (Krauss & Sales, 2014, p. 123). Further, doctoral programs generate well-rounded psychologists who are adept at integrating research and clinical work, which is often referred to as the scientist-practitioner model of training. Like master's programs, doctoral curricula include a heavy focus on coursework, requiring courses in research design, statistics, and foundational psychology topics. However, doctoral programs provide much more extensive training in foundational psychology topics and must offer instruction in certain topic areas to meet American Psychological Association (APA) accreditation standards.

TOPIC AREAS OF INSTRUCTION FOR AMERICAN PSYCHOLOGICAL ASSOCIATION ACCREDITATION

- Biological bases of behavior
- Cognitive psychology
- Social psychology
- History and systems of psychology
- Developmental psychology
- Individual differences in behavior
- Psychopathology
- Psychological assessment
- Psychological intervention
- Ethics
- Diversity

Another noteworthy aspect of doctoral programs is their focus on providing students with real-world clinical experience. Doctoral students gain clinical experience via placements, also referred to as practica (discussed in more detail in Chapter 6). Practica are carried out under the supervision of experienced mental health professionals and may take place in such settings as college counseling centers, outpatient mental health treatment centers, state hospitals, and correctional facilities. These experiences provide training in evidence-based treatment modalities and prepare students for the final stage of their doctoral training – the predoctoral internship. Internship usually comprises the final year of training, with students working in a clinical setting on a full-time basis for 1 year. Following internship, many individuals opt to take the Examination for Professional Practice in Psychology (EPPP), a national licensing exam designed by the Association of State and Provincial Psychology Boards (ASPPB) (discussed in Chapter 9). After passing the EPPP and completing any state-specific requirements (typically another test, payment of fees, and completion of paperwork), individuals become licensed psychologists who are qualified for independent clinical practice in a particular state.

There are two main types of doctoral programs in psychology: PhD and PsyD. Both degrees set graduates on track to become licensed psychologists. However, the degrees differ in their training focus. PsyD programs are focused primarily on training students to provide scientifically grounded (also referred to as empirically supported or evidence-based) clinical services. Although they may require students to complete a research project, there is considerably less focus on research in PsyD programs. Instead, clinical work is more heavily emphasized, with students often beginning their practicum placements in their first year of the program. PsyD programs may also offer a wider array of intervention-based courses. In contrast, PhD programs provide more balanced training in research and clinical work. Practicum placements begin in the first or second year of PhD training, and scientific research training is simultaneously incorporated. A wider array of statistical and research methodology course offerings is provided, and one or two formal research projects (theses and/or dissertations) are required for graduation. Additionally, PhD programs often require students to gain teaching experience.

Two other ways in which PsyD and PhD programs may differ are in their selectivity and cost of attendance. Many PhD programs offer partial or full tuition remission in addition to a stipend (i.e., funding to support cost-of-living expenses), which significantly reduces the cost of earning a PhD. Such a reduced cost comes with a trade-off. PhD programs are generally highly selective, receiving large numbers of applicants but selecting small cohorts of students. In contrast, most PsyD programs provide less financial support to their students, allowing them to admit larger cohorts. Research indicates that PhD programs (depending on their emphasis; i.e., research vs. practice-oriented) accept 7–16% of applicants, while PsyD programs (depending on their structure: freestanding vs. university professional school vs. university psychology department) accept 26–50% of applicants (Norcross, Ellis, & Sayette, 2010). Graduate program completion time may also vary, with PsyD programs taking approximately 4–6 years to complete and PhD programs taking approximately 5–7 years to complete.

Joint-Degree Programs

Both master's degrees and clinical psychology doctoral degrees help to prepare graduates to conduct research and provide psychological services that may impact the legal system. For those looking to gain a solid working knowledge of the legal system, however, a joint-degree program may be a good choice. However, although some legal knowledge is necessary to practice forensic psychology, a law degree is not necessary; the vast majority of forensic psychologists do not have formal legal training. Joint-degree programs allow students to gain the research and clinical work that master's and doctoral programs provide, while also becoming well versed in legal theory and practice. As such, they are tailored to individuals who wish to contribute to mental health policy, legal research, and the advancement of forensic psychology.

There are two main combinations of joint-degree programs. The first joint-degree combination is a JD (or law degree) with a master's degree or doctoral degree. If pursued on its own, a law degree typically takes 3 years to complete. In the first year of law school, students complete foundational coursework regarding topics such as legal writing, torts, contracts, civil procedure, constitutional law, criminal law, and property. In subsequent years of law school, students complete mainly elective coursework and participate in extracurricular activities, including law review (editing a school's law journal), moot court (appellate advocacy), or trial team (mock trial). Additionally, students at some law schools have opportunities to gain field experience by completing internships during the school year, and most law students seek field experience through summer jobs. Following completion of law school, many students opt to take the Bar Exam. Passage of the Bar Exam confers the status of esquire (and the ability to use the professional title "attorney"), allowing individuals to practice law in the jurisdiction in which they passed the Bar Exam.

Students pursuing a JD in combination with a master's degree or doctoral degree complete all the requirements to graduate from law school in conjunction with all requirements of either the master's degree or doctoral degree. As such, the completion time for both degrees is extended by 1 or 2 years, although overall completion time for such programs tends to be shorter than the time it would take to obtain both degrees individually. Although all joint-degree programs require students to complete the graduation requirements for both degrees, the sequencing of work and the integration of the curriculum are highly variable among programs. Further, funding for joint-degree programs differs greatly among programs. Some programs provide funding packages similar to that of PhD programs, with full tuition remission for both degrees and a stipend. Other programs may provide only partial funding or even no funding; in these programs, joint-degree programs may cost substantially more than pursuing a single degree.

Another joint-degree option is the MLS degree with a master's or doctoral psychology degree. The MLS degree gives students a generalized overview of the field of law. The goal of an MLS degree is not to produce individuals who are qualified to practice law, but to provide students with foundational legal knowledge that will help them to function in fields that require an understanding of the law. MLS programs also provide a solid option for individuals looking to hone their critical thinking skills. MLS degrees can typically be completed in 1 year, which substantially reduces the cost of a legal education for those who would like legal knowledge but have no interest in practicing law.

Other Types of Programs to Consider

Although the aforementioned programs represent the most common training paths for those interested in forensic psychology, there are several other training paths. First, some individuals choose to pursue non-clinical doctoral degrees. There are a variety of non-clinical areas of psychology (or closely related fields) that are relevant to forensic psychology, including legal psychology, criminology, social psychology, cognitive psychology, experimental psychology, and developmental psychology.

Second, some individuals choose to pursue clinically oriented doctoral degrees in fields related to psychology, such as a PhD in counseling psychology or EdD. The training in PhD in counseling psychology or EdD programs is substantially similar to that of doctoral programs in clinical psychology, and it is designed to produce well-rounded professionals who can thrive in research and clinical settings. However, each has a unique focus. For doctoral degrees in counseling psychology, the training focuses on how people function both individually and in relationships. There is a key distinction between a clinical psychology degree and a counseling psychology degree. Although some would argue that the distinction is slight, clinical psychology focuses on mental health disorders and behavioral health, while counseling psychology focuses on multicultural training and holistic approaches to assessment and treatment (Price, 2009). In general, clinical psychologists tend to work primarily with individuals with serious mental illness to reduce their symptoms, whereas counseling psychologists tend to work with healthy populations to improve overall life satisfaction. A Doctor of Education degree, as its name suggests, focuses on conducting research on the educational system as a whole. Completion of either a doctoral program in education or counseling psychology typically makes individuals eligible to become licensed clinicians.

As you may have noticed, there are several training paths you can take to become a forensic psychologist. So how exactly does one approach the daunting task of choosing which training road to take? The next section provides some things to consider in sorting through which degree to pursue and identifying which schools might provide the best fit.

CHOOSING THE RIGHT DEGREE

What degree should you pursue? That is certainly an important question that needs to be answered before pursuing graduate training. As with any major life decision, picking a graduate degree to pursue – a pursuit that could take anywhere from 2 to 7+ years – can be challenging. After all, how do prospective students even know where to start? What factors should be considered?

Factors to Consider in Choosing a Degree

COMMON CONSIDERATIONS IN CHOOSING WHICH DEGREE TO PURSUE

- Desired experiences and opportunities
- Desired jobs after graduation
- Financial limitations
- Duration of program
- Competitiveness of application
- Desire to complete (either immediately or eventually) a doctoral program

---

What types of experiences and opportunities do you want in graduate school? Each of the programs described above provides different types of experiences and opportunities. Nearly all offer some level of basic research design and statistics exposure, making them attractive options for individuals interested in conducting research in graduate school. However, those who are interested in more comprehensive research and statistics training/experience should target doctoral programs with a research focus, such as PhD or EdD programs. Similarly, individuals interested in clinical work or teaching opportunities might want to shy away from master's programs, unless those master's programs specifically require or offer the opportunity for clinical work or teaching. Those interested in focusing almost exclusively on clinical work during graduate school might benefit from targeting PsyD programs, where clinical work often starts during the first year. Non-clinical PhD programs also provide little opportunity for clinical work, although teaching experience may be more plentiful. Of note, exceptions apply to all of the above, so doing some independent exploration to determine which programs offer the opportunities of most interest to you is of vital importance.

Individuals with higher levels of legal interest might consider a joint-degree program. Those looking to gain a generalized view of the law to help strengthen their psychology practice might do well to target the MLS degree, while those with an interest in gaining a more comprehensive view of the law or a desire to practice law should target JD programs. JD programs provide a greater variety of coursework than MLS programs and enable students to hone legal writing and legal practice skills, and JD programs (but not MLS programs) also prepare graduates for the practice of law.

What type of job opportunities do you want after graduation? The type of training students receive is directly related to the jobs they will be eligible for upon graduation. In general, the higher the level of the degree, or the greater the number of degrees, the greater the breadth of job opportunities. For example, a doctoral degree generally confers more opportunities than a master's degree, while joint degrees open opportunities in both law and psychology. Additionally, the type of degree obtained matters; individuals obtaining degrees that allow for licensure – and hence independent clinical work – may have more opportunities than those who do not obtain such a degree. In-depth discussion of licensure and career opportunities can be found in Chapters 9 and 10, respectively.

Do you have any financial limitations? Obtaining a graduate degree can be expensive, particularly when factoring in costs already incurred to make individuals competitive for a graduate program (e.g., completing an undergraduate degree, taking Graduate Record Examinations). To this end, PhD programs have an advantage over other types of programs. Many PhD and EdD programs include either full or partial funding for tuition and a stipend. In comparison, PsyD and terminal master's degree programs typically do not provide tuition remission or stipends.

How much time are you willing to spend? Most readers are probably familiar with the adage "time is money." Applied in the context of graduate study in forensic psychology, this adage has a complex meaning. In economic terms, each year spent in graduate study comes at the opportunity cost of being able to work – it is extremely difficult to hold a job while in graduate school; in fact, some schools expressly prohibit holding an outside job while in graduate school. As such, completing a shorter-duration program allows individuals to enter the workforce earlier.

An important point to keep in mind when considering the length of a program relates back to the consideration of how much the program costs. Some programs offer tuition remission and a stipend to students. In essence, students in these programs are paid to obtain their degrees. Though they may not be making the same amount of money they could make in the workforce and will have to wait longer to enter the workforce, they are also not actively incurring significant debt.

Are you a competitive applicant? This is one of the more practical questions to consider. Although it is becoming more commonplace, obtaining a graduate degree in any field is still not the norm – its attainment represents a significant accomplishment connoting a specialized skillset. All of which is to say that getting into graduate school is difficult! All types of graduate programs in psychology require students to demonstrate some form of academic potential, typically measured by performance during college, performance on standardized tests, and research or clinical experience. Therefore, in selecting programs for which a student might be competitive, it is helpful to engage in an objective analysis of performance.

Due to their highly selective nature, clinical PhD programs tend to have the highest standards of admission. This means that students are expected to demonstrate high scores on standardized tests, high undergraduate grade point averages (GPAs), and a substantial amount of research experience (at least relative to other applicants), along with strong letters of recommendation (from supervisors, professors, bosses, etc.). As such, students lacking in any of these areas might consider addressing any shortcomings before applying – typically by retaking a standardized test and/or obtaining a job that provides research or clinical experience – lest they risk both disappointment and wasting money on application fees. In comparison, EdD, PsyD, and some non-clinical doctoral programs are less selective, although still extremely competitive. Master's programs present the lowest barrier to entry. Undergraduate GPA and standardized test scores still play a role, but admission is less competitive than in clinical PhD programs.

Are you set on getting a PhD or other doctoral degree? As noted previously, a master's degree can be pursued in a terminal master's program or as an intermediate step towards a doctoral degree. The major difference is that obtaining a master's degree as a terminal degree is much more expensive than obtaining a master's along the way to a PhD because PhD programs are usually funded (meaning the master's degree is free!). As such, for individuals set on pursuing a PhD or other doctoral degree, it may not make sense to first complete a terminal master's program, unless that master's program is being used to address weaknesses that are preventing an individual from being competitive for doctoral programs.

PICKING THE RIGHT SCHOOL

Now that you have a sense of how to pick the right type of degree program, we can get into the real nitty-gritty – how do you choose which schools to apply to? This question can be even more anxiety-provoking than the question of what type of degree to pursue, primarily because there are so many more options. But again, not to worry – we will provide some food for thought to help make the decision a little bit easier.

KEY CONSIDERATIONS IN CHOOSING THE RIGHT SCHOOL

- Desire for specialized training in graduate school
- Research interests
- APA accreditation status
- Funding/financial assistance
- Location

Are you looking for specialized training at the graduate level? This question might seem like a no-brainer – of course you are looking for some level of specialized training. After all, why else would you choose to get even more education? Indeed, it is true that all graduate programs provide specialized training, but the major question here is whether that training is more generalized or focused. There are many paths towards a career in forensic psychology. Forensic psychology is a subfield of psychology, meaning that individuals interested in pursuing a career in forensic psychology must first receive general psychological training. According to the APA, a "specialty" is a "defined area of professional psychology practice characterized by a distinctive configuration of competent services for specified problems and populations" (APA, 2011, p. 2). APA first recognized forensic psychology as a specialty area in 2001, noting that it is defined by "activities primarily intended to provide professional psychology expertise within the judicial and legal systems" (APA, n.d.a). According to the APA's *Principles for the Recognition of Specialties in Professional Psychology*, specialty training can occur at either the doctoral or postdoctoral levels (or both!) (APA, 2011).

TEN MAJOR TOPIC AREAS OF FORENSIC COURSEWORK

(Burl et al., 2012)

- Introductory/general forensic psychology
- Forensic assessment
- Forensic treatment
- Social psychology and the law
- Psychology of criminal behavior
- Juvenile offending
- Mental health law
- Victimology
- Ethical issues in forensic psychology
- Socio-cultural issues in forensic psychology

There are a few things to consider for those interested in obtaining forensic experience during their doctoral training. First, it is important to identify schools that offer specialized forensic training. This is usually accomplished through the offering of courses relevant to psychology and law. Doctoral programs offering specialized forensic coursework may also require completion of a research project – a thesis and/or dissertation – addressing a forensic psychological topic.

Second, it is helpful to identify which schools might have access to forensic populations as part of practicum experiences. As you will learn in graduate school, practicum training is just as important as, if not more important than, coursework. Courses typically provide the foundation necessary to understand a topic, while practica allow individuals to practice and hone their skills in the real world. Programs that provide practica with forensic populations provide a valuable training opportunity for future forensic psychologists, even if there is no formal instruction on forensic psychology in the program's curriculum. Common practicum placements that may offer access to forensic populations include jails/

prisons, juvenile placement facilities, state hospitals, forensic hospitals, and private practices. Of note, however, it is not necessary to work in a forensic or correctional setting to work with patients with juvenile or criminal histories. In fact, a survey by Morgan and colleagues (2007) found that, although only 26% of graduate students in clinical or counseling psychology doctoral programs completed placements in a correctional or forensic setting, high percentages of students across all types of practicum placements reported having had a current or recent client who had a juvenile history, had been charged with a crime, had been incarcerated, or met criteria for antisocial personality disorder.

Another consideration in identifying programs that provide forensic training during graduate school is whether the school has any professors with a forensic psychology background. One way to obtain specialized training in forensic psychology is to be mentored by a forensic psychologist – this can happen in graduate school or post-graduation. Many programs may not offer more formal specialized training in forensic psychology, but they might have a faculty member who does forensic clinical work or conducts forensic research. To this end, a student may attend a program that provides generalized psychological training, but obtain forensic mentorship from a particular faculty member with a forensic background. An easy way to identify schools that have faculty with forensic interests is to conduct searches for research articles related to forensic psychology and note the authors' institutional affiliations.

What are your research interests? Your research interests represent another integral cog in the program selection wheel. As noted, forensic psychology is a huge subfield of psychology, encompassing many areas of overlap between psychology and the legal system. To this end, students' research interests play a substantial role in program selection. For example, students with an interest in juvenile justice may want to target programs with faculty members that have juvenile justice research or practice interests. A good way to identify researchers who share your interests is to search for articles on a particular topic area, note the authors' institutional affiliations, and then check the institution website to see if they have a psychology graduate program or a graduate program in a related subfield.

Is the program accredited? To maximize the influence and weight of your degree, it is important to seek out doctoral programs that are accredited by the APA. Accreditation is the process by which the APA ensures that a graduate program meets the minimum requirements to produce competent psychologists who can be trusted to practice independently. APA accreditation serves as the most widely recognized quality control measure that signals that a doctoral program meets standards for training and education in the field of professional psychology (APA, n.d.b). APA only accredits doctoral programs, although master's programs may be accredited by a regional accreditation organization. Attending a non-accredited program may limit your ability to apply to an extensive range of internship sites (because some internships require attendance at an APA-accredited program), and some states require graduation from an APA-accredited program to become licensed.

Do you have concerns about funding and location? This factor is highly relevant in choosing a graduate program. Many graduate students are married, in long-term relationships, or have other family obligations that would make relocation very difficult, while others may be in a challenging financial situation and concerned about accruing more debt. Still others may want to attend graduate school in an area that they have chosen to be their permanent home. Whatever the situation, location and funding play a huge role in selecting programs that require large time and effort commitments, particularly during some of life's most formative years.

What resources can help students identify programs that best fit their needs? As with anything, there are more efficient and less efficient ways to identify which schools might best fit your needs. Internet searches for "forensic psychology" or "clinical psychology" programs will turn up lots of results, but it would be challenging to sift through each website to determine if those programs truly offer the forensic experience you seek. Fortunately, APA has an annual publication titled *Graduate Study in Psychology* that contains information about graduate programs in psychology, including the program's application requirements, admission rates, tuition costs, student outcome information, theoretical orientation, and research emphases. Additionally, the APA website has a useful search tool for APA-accredited clinically oriented programs (www.apa.org/ed/accreditation/programs/index.aspx), which enables prospective students to sift through programs by program focus (e.g., clinical psychology, counseling psychology, school psychology) and search for keywords, such as "forensic psychology."

There is an even more specific resource for those interested in forensic psychology. Each year, the American Psychology-Law Society (AP-LS), which is Division 41 of APA, revises its *Guide to Graduate Programs in Forensic and Legal Psychology*. This resource catalogs all programs that have a specific law–psychology focus and categorizes them by program type (master's, PhD, PsyD, or joint degree). This guide details the types of degree the school offers, the number of applications received per year, admissions requirements, funding information, research focus, clinical work expectations, and the types of jobs graduates obtain. As of 2018, AP-LS identified 23 PhD programs, six PsyD programs, eight joint-degree programs, and 25 master's programs that have a law–psychology focus. The AP-LS guide can be found at the following link: www.apadivisions.org/division-41/education/programs/index.aspx.

★ ★ ★

CONCLUSION

The goals of this chapter were to provide an overview of the different types of graduate training programs available to those interested in forensic psychology, and to discuss the many considerations that are relevant when determining what type of training program and institution to attend. The main takeaways of the chapter are:

- There are many types of graduate programs that provide a strong foundation in forensic psychology. These include master's programs; PhD programs in clinical, counseling, or social psychology; PsyD programs; EdD programs; and joint-degree programs.
- Each program has advantages and disadvantages. Terminal master's degree programs are shorter, providing only a generalized overview of psychology, and allow for quicker entry into the workforce, but they may not provide a clear path to becoming a licensed psychologist and are also typically not funded. Doctoral programs take longer to complete but include a stronger focus on research (PhD programs) and clinical work (PhD and PsyD programs). Typically, students in PhD programs and most EdD programs do not pay tuition (or at least not full tuition) and receive a stipend, whereas students in PsyD programs typically pay full tuition.
- There are many factors to consider in choosing the right graduate school for you, including the type of training experience you would like to have in graduate school, your research interests, whether the program is accredited, and if you have financial or geographic restrictions.
- There are several resources that can assist you to identify programs that offer training in forensic psychology. These resources include APA's *Graduate Study in Psychology*, the APA website's program search tool, and AP-LS's *Guide to Graduate Programs in Forensic and Legal Psychology*.

REFERENCES

American Psychological Association. (2011, August). *Principles for the recognition of specialties in professional psychology.* Retrieved on July 19, 2019 from www.apa.org/about/policy/principles-recognition.pdf

American Psychological Association. (n.d.a). *Forensic psychology.* Retrieved on July 19, 2019 from www.apa.org/ed/graduate/specialize/forensic.aspx

American Psychological Association. (n.d.b). *Guidelines and principles for accreditation of programs in professional psychology: Quick reference guide to doctoral programs.* Retrieved on July 19, 2019 from www.apa.org/ed/accreditation/about/policies/doctoral.aspx

Burl, J., Shah, S., Filone, S., Foster, E., & DeMatteo, D. (2012). A survey of graduate training programs and coursework in forensic psychology. *Teaching of Psychology, 39,* 48–53.

Krauss, D. A., & Sales, B. (2014). Training in forensic psychology. In I. B. Weiner & R. K. Otto (Eds.), *Handbook of forensic psychology* (4th ed., pp. 111–134). Hoboken, NJ: Wiley.

Morgan, R. D., Beer, A. M., Fitzgerald, K. L., & Mandracchia, J. T. (2007). Graduate students' experiences, interests, and attitudes toward correctional/forensic psychology. *Criminal Justice and Behavior, 34,* 96–107.

Norcross, J. C., Ellis, J. L., & Sayette, M. A. (2010). Getting in and getting money: A comparative analysis of admission standards, acceptance rates, and financial assistance across the research-practice continuum in clinical psychology programs. *Training and Education in Professional Psychology, 4,* 99–104.

Price, M. (2009, March). Counseling vs. clinical programs: Similarities abound. *GradPSYCH, 7*(2), 6.

FURTHER READING

American Psychological Association. (n.d.). *Choosing a program.* Retrieved on July 19, 2019 from www.apa.org/ed/accreditation/about/program-choice.aspx

American Psychological Association. (n.d.). *Counseling vs. clinical programs: Similarities abound.* Retrieved on July 19, 2019 from www.apa.org/gradpsych/2009/03/similarities.aspx

American Psychological Association. (n.d.) *Pursuing a career in social psychology.* Retrieved on July 19, 2019 from www.apa.org/action/science/social/education-training.aspx

American Psychological Association. (2017). *Graduate study in psychology, 2018 edition.* Washington, DC: Author.

Bersoff, D., Goodman-Delahunty, J., Grisso, J. T., Hans, V., Poythress, Jr., N. G., & Roesch, R.G. (1997). Training in law and psychology: Models from the Villanova Conference. *American Psychologist, 52,* 1301–1310.

DeMatteo, D., Marczyk, G., Krauss, D. A., & Burl, J. (2009). Educational and training models in forensic psychology. *Training and Education in Professional Psychology, 3,* 184–191.

Differences between PhD, PsyD, and EdD. (2015, November). Retrieved on July 19, 2019 from www.professionaldevelopmentpath.com/differences-between-phd-psyd-and-edd/

Michalski, D. S., & Fowler, G. (2016, January). *Doctoral degrees in psychology: How are they different, or not so different?* Retrieved from www.apa.org/ed/precollege/psn/2016/01/doctoral-degrees.aspx

Zaitchik, M., Berman, G., Whitworth, D., & Platania, J. (2013). The time is now: The emerging need for master's level training in forensic psychology. *Journal of Forensic Psychology Practice, 7*, 65–71.

CHAPTER 5

Applications and Interviews

Helpful Hints for Maximizing Your Chances of Graduate Admission

By now, you probably have a sense of how best to structure your undergraduate and post-college years to strengthen yourself as a candidate for graduate admission. You also may have begun to narrow down your list of programs with the help of the resources provided in Chapter 4. All that is left to do is apply!

Easier said than done. The graduate school application process is competitive, complex, and lengthy. The anxiety that comes with the application process can be a powerful deterrent from getting started. In this chapter, we walk you through the application and interview process and discuss what to do if you are not accepted. Although we will touch briefly upon other degree options (identified in Chapters 3 and 4),[1] we will focus on applied doctoral programs because they are considered entry-level degrees (i.e., the minimum professional degree required for employment) for a career in forensic psychology.

It is important to keep in mind that the graduate school application process is competitive for *everyone*. Unfortunately, a strong academic background and impressive professional experience do not guarantee admission into graduate school. However, being knowledgeable about relevant considerations and having tips at your disposal may help to maximize your chances of success.

FIRST IMPRESSIONS: THE APPLICATION PROCESS

The entirety of the application process serves as one big first impression. For most applicants, this is the initial point of contact with the programs that they hope to attend. Think carefully about the future career that you hope to build for yourself and the characteristics you want to present to prospective mentors during each step of the process.

In **mentor-based programs**, prospective students apply to work directly with a specific faculty member whose research and clinical interests closely match theirs. The mentor-based model is common in clinical PhD programs.

It can be challenging to figure out when and where to start. As described in Chapter 4, the selection of preferred programs is influenced by several factors that gauge overall "fit," including opportunities for specialized training, research interests, associated faculty, program accreditation, funding opportunities, and geographic location. One major consideration is whether the program is mentor-based, an approach that allows applicants to prioritize receiving specialized training in forensic psychology as a graduate student. Applying to approximately 10 clinical PhD programs is a solid general guideline, with a mix of "reach" schools and more realistic options, as indicated by test scores and grade point average (GPA) (Geher, 2017). The American Psychological Association's (APA's) annually published *Graduate Study in Psychology* and the American Psychology-Law Society's *Guide to Graduate Programs in Forensic and Legal Psychology* are great springboards to help you compare programs and narrow down your lists.

Once applicants generate a list of programs, they can begin compiling materials and gathering information about each program's application process. Deadlines will vary based on the school, so it is prudent to note them well in advance. In general, doctoral program application deadlines are in mid to late fall of the year prior to starting the program, and deadlines for master's program applications are typically several months later.

Unlike the Common Application, an online platform widely used by high school students to apply to multiple undergraduate institutions in a systematic fashion, each graduate school typically has a distinct application. However, APA recently developed a Centralized Application Service (PSYCAS) that streamlines the process of applying to master's and doctoral programs in psychology. PSYCAS manages correspondence between programs and applicants, distributes applicant transcripts to target schools, provides status updates, and offers customer service. At the time of this publication, Palo Alto University is the only forensic program that uses this service (APA, n.d.).

Components of the Application

Applications for graduate programs in psychology typically include several components: (1) applicant background information, such as contact information and educational history; (2) a curriculum vitae (CV)/resume that cites relevant research and clinical experience, skills, and achievements (e.g., awards, publications); (3) test scores, transcripts, and GPAs from all prior schools (after high school); (4) letters of recommendation; and (5) personal statements (Hayes & Hayes, 1989). Although less common, some programs will request a writing sample, which is often research-based (e.g., honors thesis), but may be clinical (e.g., evaluation report, case conceptualization).

To maximize chances of success, Graduate Record Examinations (GRE) scores must be competitive. Most clinical doctoral programs provide information regarding minimum requirements, ranges, and average GPA and GRE scores for each of the past few incoming cohorts (Prinstein, 2017). These data enable prospective students to gauge their likelihood of acceptance and to potentially remediate observed shortcomings. Prospective applicants whose GRE scores are not competitive may benefit from retaking the test prior to applying. There are a handful of test preparation materials and courses for students looking for additional help with raising their GRE scores.

Additionally, CVs/resumes should be carefully edited and well crafted to highlight applicants' accomplishments in a concise and accurate manner. Although it is not necessary to have completed an undergraduate degree prior to the application deadline, as is the case for those applying to graduate school during their final year of college, a bachelor's degree must be conferred by the time students begin their graduate training. Although the application process is substantially similar across most doctoral programs, there are always exceptions. We cannot stress enough the importance of careful research to identify each program's specific requirements, which are typically made available on admission websites.

LETTERS OF RECOMMENDATION

Selecting the Right Reference

Letters of recommendation are a critical component of the graduate school application. They are a personalized and detailed account of an applicant's potential as a graduate student above and beyond what admissions committees glean from test scores, grades, and CVs. Furthermore, they provide insight into an applicant as an employee, colleague, clinician, researcher, and – importantly – as a person. Graduate schools typically require two or three references (i.e., individuals who have agreed to write a letter of recommendation or to be contacted by programs to speak to the applicant's qualifications), but they may request or allow for submission of more letters. Some programs also specify *who* should serve as a reference, requesting letters from a mix of psychologists, professors, and/or researchers.

TIPS FOR SELECTING THE RIGHT REFERENCE

- Plan ahead
- Choose a "strong" reference
- Make relevant selections
- Aim for variety
- Be objective and professional

Plan Ahead

If you know well in advance that you plan to apply to graduate school, then you should be thinking about who might ultimately serve as a potential reference as you seek research or clinical positions and complete relevant coursework. How do you want to portray yourself to the admissions committee and to a potential mentor? Act accordingly in the context of any experience from which you think you will request a letter of recommendation.

Choose a "Strong" Reference

Select carefully. A reference should be able to attest to your abilities *beyond* what the application already reveals. For example, it does not convey much if a reference is only able to say that a student earned an A+ in his or her advanced psychology course, or that a research assistant's responsibilities included X, Y, and Z; these details are likely referenced elsewhere in the application. Additionally, it is not always valuable to obtain a recommendation from the most influential name if he or she cannot also make a compelling case for your acceptance and meaningfully address your qualifications, unique contributions, and favorable characteristics (Clark, 2009).

Make Relevant Selections

If possible, try to obtain a reference that can address each of the relevant domains for clinical doctoral programs: academic, research, and clinical. This can be challenging, particularly if you are applying as an undergraduate student. In these cases, think carefully about whether your skills and responsibilities from one realm can easily translate to another. For example, although you may not have had the opportunity to work in a research lab, perhaps you completed a brief research study for a research methods course. Similarly, although you may not have had direct clinical experience, you may have conducted phone screens to recruit individuals with psychiatric diagnoses for a research project. However, be mindful of overstating a prior experience. It may not be advisable to ask for a letter of recommendation from your manager at a summer retail job, even if your responsibilities involved "people skills."

Aim for Variety

You will have a better chance of demonstrating to prospective graduate programs that you are well rounded and will make significant contributions to the program if you seek recommendation letters from a variety of sources spanning multiple domains. For example, even if your performance in a course was outstanding, avoid obtaining recommendation letters from both your course professor and teaching assistant (TA) because there will likely be significant overlap in the content of the letters. Also, avoid having someone of the same professional status (e.g., fellow research assistant or undergraduate TA) serve as a reference because that person's letter may not hold the same value as a letter from an experienced professional.

Be Objective and Professional

You should not ask a personal contact, such as a close friend, family member, or personal doctor or therapist, to serve as a reference even if he or she works in a related field. It is unlikely that these individuals will be able to speak objectively to your qualifications in a professional context. Furthermore, choosing to do so may raise questions regarding your ability to secure a more appropriate reference who can attest to your skillset.

"Kisses of Death"

Appleby and Appleby (2006) surveyed 88 chairs of admissions committees at psychology graduate programs to identify "kisses of death" (i.e., choices that increase the likelihood of a program rejecting an otherwise competitive applicant) for prospective graduate students. In terms of letters of recommendation, they determined that inappropriate sources and undesirable applicant characteristics are the primary pitfalls.

Inappropriate sources include personal contacts who are unable to speak to an applicant's performance in a relevant professional setting. Additionally, although applicants select their own references, this does not always guarantee a positive letter of recommendation. References may be motivated to be upfront and honest as a professional courtesy, particularly if they are in the same field as a prospective mentor. Thus, admissions committees have received recommendation letters that both explicitly define and implicitly suggest undesirable applicant characteristics. These range from negative (e.g., "arrogant, not a team player, and self-centered" [p. 20]) to neutral and sparse (e.g., "lack of superlatives" [p. 20]) (Appleby & Appleby, 2006).

How to Approach a Potential Reference

Now that you have a sense of the types of recommendation letters you would like to receive and from whom, the next step is to request them. This may seem like a minor consideration given the range of things to think about when applying to graduate school, but remember that the entire application process is your first impression! Selecting and approaching potential references in an organized, timely, and thoughtful manner is an opportunity to demonstrate the positive attributes you would like to be reflected in your recommendation letters.

Make Your References' Jobs Easier

Organization is critical to success as an applicant. Provide your references with a copy of your CV and a list of programs, including relevant information such as the degree and major area of study (e.g., forensic) you are applying for, deadlines, and instructions for how to submit the recommendation (Clark, 2009). Be sure to remind them of notable accomplishments from your time working together.

Be Considerate of Timelines (Theirs and Yours)

Doctoral applications are typically due in late fall, which is a busy time of year for professors. If your references are professors, they are also likely providing letters for other applicants. Give letter writers sufficient advance notice about the due date for the letter; asking for a letter to be written within a few days or even a few weeks typically does not give the letter writer sufficient time to draft a comprehensive letter, and those types of time-pressured requests may not be well received by potential letter writers.

Follow Up

Reach out to your references as the deadline approaches and monitor the program's application portal for updates regarding submission of recommendation letters (Clark, 2009). This step can quickly turn into a last-minute scramble to meet the deadline, and it is your responsibility to ensure that it is done successfully.

PERSONAL STATEMENTS

The personal statement (also referred to as a statement of interest or letter of intent) is a central component of graduate applications and a critical way to "sell yourself" as an applicant. The personal statement is often the most challenging aspect of the application process. They can vary greatly from program to program both in terms of word limits (ranging anywhere from 500 to 1,500 words) and desired content. However, a personal statement typically assumes the form of a narrative, including discussion of relevant experience (research, clinical, and academic), qualifications, goals for graduate school, and future career plans. For doctoral programs, and occasionally for master's programs, the personal statement will also include mention of specific faculty with whom the applicant would like to work while in graduate school (Hogan, 2016).

The personal statement should be tailored to the specific program. If the program is mentor-based, the personal statement is your chance to high-light your shared interests with a specific faculty member. It is important to emphasize and clearly establish your fit with the field of forensic psychology and the specific graduate program. This is also an opportunity to demonstrate your skills as a writer. Remember that admissions committees and faculty members have busy schedules, and your application is likely one of many (possibly hundreds!) of applications they will read. The more compelling and articulate you can make your personal statement, the better your chances of gaining admission.

Tips and Considerations

Knowing where to start or how to best maximize your chances of impressing the admissions committee with a strong personal statement can be difficult. To further complicate things, programs or faculty members will be looking for different features in these essays, and it is difficult to know exactly what those are. There is no cookie-cutter formula for crafting the perfect personal statement, but there are a few considerations to keep in mind.

TIPS FOR CRAFTING YOUR PERSONAL STATEMENT

- Do not use the same statement for all programs
- Create a skeleton (or template) statement
- Venture beyond the content of your curriculum vitae
- Focus on what you *learned*
- Capture your "fit" with the program
- Address gaps in your story
- Demonstrate knowledge of the field
- Carefully consider whether to include a personal anecdote
- Be thorough
- Proofread, proofread, proofread!

Do Not Use the Same Statement for All Programs

Although it is likely that much of the content remains the same – particularly if you have a clear idea of what you hope to study – statements should be personalized to each school (Hogan, 2016). If you are identifying specific faculty members with whom you would like to work, tailor your stated interests to closely match theirs and introduce something new or unique (e.g., an interesting perspective on or secondary hypothesis for ongoing research). In addition to conveying why you want to become a forensic psychologist, the committee wants to know why you want to do so at their university. Does the program's clinical training focus on a theoretical orientation that is particularly relevant to the work you want to do as a forensic psychologist? Does its location afford you access to the types of populations with whom you wish to work? Does the program have a faculty member with whom you would be a good professional fit?

But Create a Skeleton

Although we just outlined the many reasons not to reuse the same personal statement, it is acceptable to operate from a general skeleton or template. You do not need to reinvent the wheel with every graduate application.

In reality, your general research interests and career goals will not differ greatly from program to program. As such, much of the base content may stay the same, despite program-specific alterations.

Venture Beyond What Is on Your CV

The personal statement should not simply be a regurgitation of your CV. Instead, highlight a few relevant, unique, and formative experiences and find creative ways to concisely reference other qualifications. For example, few individuals obtain clinical experience with forensic populations prior to graduate school, so such experience would be worth discussing in a personal statement if an applicant managed to obtain that type of experience. Attending an undergraduate institution known for its forensic training is also a meaningful experience; however, given word limits, it would be wasteful to list every forensic course you took because this information is available on your transcript. Instead, you might find a way to note your relevant academic background in a couple of sentences before transitioning to something else deserving of mention.

Focus on What You Learned, Not Just What You Did

Remember that the goal of these statements is to distinguish yourself from the many other qualified applicants. Their lists of skills and experiences likely mirror yours. Therefore, focus on what you learned and what those experiences generated. Did you develop any hypotheses based on observations from the research project you worked on? Were you able to develop an observation into a side research project? Focusing on these things is a way to make your application stand out.

"Fit" Is Foremost

Admissions committees are interested in applicants who are a good fit for their program (Hogan, 2016). This may refer to your research and/or clinical interests, career aspirations, and desire for specific training experiences. For example, if a clinical PhD program expects students to acquire grants, complete multiple independent research projects, and become leading researchers in the field, you are unlikely to be a good fit if you have no research experience and are solely interested in clinical work. If you are interested in behavioral therapy with juvenile offenders and the program only provides training from a psychodynamic perspective, then the program may not be a good fit for you. For mentor-based programs, fit with the research interests and opportunities available through that specific faculty member is of paramount importance. You can still be a competitive applicant even if your interests and background do not map perfectly on to those of a program or specific faculty member, but if you find yourself stretching the truth or having to invent interests for the purpose of your personal statement, it will probably be obvious to the admissions committee and faculty. It is also worth considering whether it is a program worth applying to given available time, effort, and money.

Address Gaps in Your Story

Think critically about any gaps in your educational and professional history (e.g., the 3 years after college that are not accounted for on your CV) or questions that may arise (e.g., having an undergraduate degree in a field other than psychology). You may also want to briefly and objectively address a non-competitive GPA if you have a compelling reason for this shortcoming (e.g., low freshman year GPA due to entering college as a physics major before switching majors to psychology). Lastly, if you have some unrelated experiences, connect the dots to clearly convey your interest in the field of forensic psychology.

Demonstrate Direction and Knowledge of the Field

Graduate programs do not typically expect applicants to have already solidified their dissertation topic, but it is helpful to your candidacy if you can demonstrate a general area of interest (e.g., novel treatments for juvenile offenders) and generate a few potential directions of study (e.g., whether therapy differentially impacts male and female juvenile offenders). Additionally, the personal statement is a useful opportunity to convey your understanding of the field of forensic psychology and professional routes to pursue within it. We will come back to this important point shortly.

Weigh the Value of a Personal Anecdote

Writing a creative statement or setting yourself apart as an applicant is sometimes associated with sharing a personal anecdote. Although this is not necessarily a bad idea, think carefully about the impression you want to make to the admissions committee and how impactful an anecdote might be given the goals of your personal statement. An additional consideration is whether an anecdote may reveal a limited understanding of the field of forensic psychology. For example, although tempting – and certainly something that would make you stand out – it may not be advantageous, relevant, or even unique to discuss your documented efforts to solve the JonBenét Ramsey case over the years, how your under-graduate course Criminals Throughout American History equipped you with the knowledge to contribute to criminal profiling and crime scene investigations, or personal experiences as a victim or perpetrator of crime. However, an anecdote about working with justice-involved populations could be both compelling and relevant.

Be Thorough

Make sure that you address each required aspect of the personal statement per the instructions provided on the program's website. You should also touch upon each of the salient focuses of the program. For example, if the school equally emphasizes research and clinical training, it would not be wise to use almost all your allotted words to discuss why research is the only thing you have ever wanted to do.

Proofread, Proofread, Proofread!

And have others proofread. Your personal statement is not the place to make simple typos – or bigger ones, like referencing X University in a personal statement submitted to Y University, or misspelling the name of the faculty member with whom you want to work. (We have seen both of these mistakes many times!) It may seem impossible to make an error on such an important component of your application, but these mistakes become increasingly likely by the tenth draft of your essay because you have become so familiar with it. Typos may suggest a lack of attention to detail or a lackadaisical approach to the competitive graduate application process. When there are many qualified candidates, avoid doing anything that can draw negative attention. Take some time away from your drafts, and then come back to them with a clear mind. You may also ask close friends, colleagues, or current supervisors to provide feedback on your statement.

More "Kisses of Death"

Appleby and Appleby (2006) identified characteristics of personal statements that have been negatively received by admissions commit-tees, including mention of personal mental health problems, excessive self-disclosure, stories about excessive altruism, and professionally inappropriate content. "Graduate school is an academic/career path, not a personal treatment or intervention for problems" (Appleby & Appleby, 2006, p. 20). Although it is fine to be motivated to pursue this career by your own experiences with mental health, your personal statement is not the place to discuss this. The decision to disclose your own mental health status may demonstrate an inability to gauge and adhere to social and professional norms. Admissions committees may view self-disclosure in a personal statement as "an indication of poor interpersonal boundaries" (Appleby & Appleby, 2006, p. 20). Additional forms of disclosure may include irrelevant and overly personal details of one's life, such as a litany of personal challenges faced during college.

It is not necessary to explicitly state that you "want to help everyone." This idea is unoriginal and likely applies to most people who pursue careers in clinical psychology. Committees also referenced applicants who included "cutesy" content or excessive and inappropriate humor in their essays (Appleby & Appleby, 2006). Additionally, avoid including references to unrelated and potentially polarizing content, such as the role of your religious beliefs in your decision to pursue graduate training in forensic psychology, or perhaps your views on the appropriateness of the death penalty.

As you may have gleaned, writing a personal statement is difficult! Prepare for it to be challenging and time consuming, and recognize that writing a personal statement requires research, careful thought, and many rounds of editing. It is difficult, but certainly possible, to make a lasting positive impression on paper.

ADDITIONAL CONSIDERATIONS

Graduate school applications consist of many moving parts that can seem overwhelming to manage. Factoring in larger-scale considerations will help organize and orient the process.

Timeline

Budgeting time effectively is critical. Programs that receive hundreds of applications may not be sympathetic to the old "dog ate my wireless router" excuse for not submitting an application by the deadline. Even if they are forgiving, the admissions committee or your prospective mentor may be informed of the late submission. This is not an ideal first impression. Managing this timeline is further complicated by the many balls you will be

juggling, including coordinating letters of recommendation, ordering transcripts, sending test scores to target programs, or even receiving test scores if
(re)taking the GRE later in the process.[2]

Geher (2017) provides a suggested timeline to promote advanced preparation
and to allot yourself enough time to devote to each step of the application
process.

Contacting Faculty Members

Some prospective students contact the faculty members with whom they
would like to work prior to submitting their application, although this
communication may be less common for programs that are not mentor-
based. Contacting a faculty member can also engender anxiety, but doing
so can set you apart from other applicants and demonstrate your interest to
a potential mentor. As with all things related to the application, contact
faculty with careful consideration. Remember, this is a (first) first impression, even before the application itself, and sending multiple e-mails or
asking too many questions may not generate a positive first impression.

Contacting faculty via e-mail is most common (Buffardi, 2014). E-mail
communication provides you with the ability to carefully craft your initial
contact and later correspondence, but it also means your communication
will be in writing, which the recipient can keep for future reference.
A few considerations can help increase your chances of making a good
impression.

When corresponding with a potential mentor before applying to a
program, do:

- Time your initial contact well. Early fall may be a good time
  because it is not so far in advance of the application deadline that
  the faculty member may forget that you were in contact and not so
  delayed that it can be perceived as an afterthought.
- Have a legitimate purpose for contacting the faculty member.
  A typical reason is to confirm whether he or she plans on accepting
  new students for the next academic year or to clarify shared interests.
  With that said, faculty members may be put off by requests from
  applicants to "tell me all of the research you are doing now and plan
  to do over the next 5 years." Some faculty members receive many
  dozens of e-mails from prospective applicants, and e-mails that

require lengthy, time-consuming responses may not create a positive first impression.

- Provide *brief* background information that is relevant and suggests that you might be a good fit, referencing the faculty member's work as appropriate.
- Attach an up-to-date CV.
- Offer to be available via e-mail or phone if he or she would like to speak further.
- Be concise; avoid overly lengthy e-mails that will take up too much of the faculty member's time.
- Thank the faculty member for his or her time.

When corresponding with a faculty member, do not:

- Ask questions that you can easily find the answer to on the program website. This will communicate that you are not thorough in your preparation, and such questions may be perceived by the faculty member as a waste of his or her time.
- Flood him or her with questions that are irrelevant or will be unnecessarily time consuming to answer. Keep in mind that other applicants will be doing the same and that faculty members have many other responsibilities.
- E-mail multiple faculty members within a department to express your interest in working with each of them. Assume that faculty speak to each other. E-mailing a professor to say that you are exclusively passionate about eating disorders and e-mailing his or her colleague at the same university to say the same about forensic psychology will reflect poorly and create confusion. This approach is appropriate for programs that allow you to work with or apply to multiple mentors, but you should still be mindful of potentially disparate reported interests and be sure to bridge the gap in a logical manner.
- Be impatient. A faculty member may not respond for any number of reasons (e.g., on sabbatical, very busy, traveling). This is not a deal breaker, but sending repeated e-mails that reflect impatience and show a lack of respect for the faculty member's time may be.
- Be overzealous or make assumptions (e.g., "Looking forward to meeting you at interviews in February!").
- Be informal.
- Text a faculty member without permission to do so. (Yes, this happens with some regularity because cell phone numbers are often included on a faculty member's CV.)

Contacting faculty members is not necessary unless specified by the program. However, it can be helpful to make contact, particularly if there is no indication of which faculty members are accepting students. If you choose to do so, proceed carefully and thoughtfully. When reviewing applications, a faculty member is more likely to remember an applicant who sent an off-putting e-mail than someone who did not reach out at all.

Finances

Budget your finances accordingly. Nearly every step of the application process involves spending money, including sending your scores and transcripts and submitting applications. Some programs offer fee waivers in select cases (e.g., for military personnel or on a needs basis, or if the application is submitted online); however, even if you fall into a relevant category, you are not guaranteed financial support. You can find information regarding fee waivers on program websites, and be sure to factor applying for the waivers into your application timeline.

THE WAITING GAME

Putting your best foot forward and submitting your applications is a big feat! Unfortunately, once your applications have been submitted and are floating around in the ether, the grueling period of waiting begins. We cannot offer you much solace except to say that thousands of other applicants are experiencing the same thing. During this period, graduate programs will be inundated with applications to review and likely will not be able to provide status updates on a particular application. Due to the large number of applications that graduate programs in psychology receive annually, applicants who are not invited to interview often will not be notified until well after the program's interview period has passed.

   If your application has impressed the program, the common next step is to be invited to interview. This is less typical for master's programs, unless the program is mentor-based. You may learn that you are being considered in one of a few ways: through the program's online application portal, an e-mail from the program or faculty, or a phone call directly from the faculty member to whom you applied. Unfortunately, there is no set date for interview offers, but programs will usually provide timelines for interviews on the admissions website.

   As mentioned, a faculty member may contact you directly by phone to invite you to interview. Take this step of the process seriously. These conversations can be brief – simply an invitation or brief update that interview details are forthcoming – or they can be a "pre-interview," in which case you may be expected to discuss your qualifications and interest in attending that program and working with the faculty member (Oudekerk & Bottoms, 2007). This is yet another opportunity to make a good long-distance impression.

LASTING IMPRESSIONS: THE INTERVIEWS

Advancing to the interview stage is a notable accomplishment and a strong indication that you have already impressed the program and faculty. It is also yet another cause of anxiety. Although it is normal to be nervous about upcoming interviews, there are steps you can take to help ease the tension and improve your chances of success on interview day. Preparation is key!

The Basics

Despite being a good problem to have, receiving interview offers from multiple schools requires the careful organization of schedules, coordination of travel, and requests for time off from work or school. This is further complicated because invitations to interview are received in a staggered fashion, so you may find yourself in a position where you have already accepted an interview and then receive another interview offer for the same day, perhaps from a program in which you are more interested. Try to avoid rescheduling as much as possible; doing so requires effort to coordinate on the program's end and can convey a relative lack of interest in that program. However, sometimes conflicts are inevitable, even with attempts to reschedule. You can either attempt to troubleshoot (e.g., conducting a Skype interview instead of attending in person) or, unfortunately, you may have to make a choice between programs and decline an interview offer. To add to the scheduling frenzy, interviews typically take place in the winter, which can be a challenging time to travel. Finally, interviewing can be expensive when you consider the cost of travel, lodging, and appropriate interview attire.

Lodging

Graduate programs understand the costs associated with applications and interviews, so they will often have deals with local hotels or offer free lodging with current graduate students. Some believe that you should definitely stay with a student if offered the option, while others believe that it will not strongly impact your chances of admission. As with much of what we have discussed in this chapter, it depends!

There are several benefits associated with staying with a graduate student, including gaining insight into the program, having more face time with current students and thus greater opportunity to demonstrate your personality, and saving money. Furthermore, a graduate student host may help to facilitate introductions to faculty members or to navigate the city or town in which the program is located.

On the other hand, interviews are inherently stressful, and staying with a graduate student in some ways acts as an extension of the interview. Feedback of your stay may be communicated to your prospective mentor, which means you should be friendly, polite, and professional at all times. Additionally, there is no guarantee regarding the amenities provided. You may be sleeping on a couch or in a sleeping bag and will be operating under someone else's schedule. If you choose formal lodging, such as a hotel, factor in details such as its distance from the program, transportation options, and check-in/check-out policies.

Ultimately, the decision to stay with a graduate student or secure other forms of lodging is based on your comfort level and finances. Staying with a student – even if you get along great – does not guarantee you will get an offer of admission. Similarly, choosing to book a hotel room or staying with friends/family does not exclude you from making a stellar impression during other stages of the process.

Interview Prep

Now that the logistics are ironed out, it is time to prepare for the interview itself. At the risk of sounding like a broken record, do your research! Begin re-familiarizing yourself with the program, including its relative focus on research and clinical work, clinical orientation (e.g., cognitive-behavioral therapy), and what makes it unique and appealing to you. For mentor-based programs, you should be familiar with the faculty member's research and how your interests overlap. Additionally, it may be beneficial, although often not expected, to briefly familiarize yourself with other faculty's areas of interest because it is not uncommon to interview with multiple people in addition to your potential mentor.

Continue updating your CV and bring a few copies with you to interview day. If notable changes have occurred since applications were due (e.g., manuscripts in preparation were published, new job experience), then you may want to provide an updated version to your interviewers.

Providing an updated CV reflects your attention to detail and highlights recent developments that may impact admissions decisions.

One of the best ways to prepare in advance of interview day is to generate questions to ask current students and faculty. These may include general questions about funding, work–life balance, geographic location, or program culture. It is also advantageous to prepare for each interview individually, generating specific topics you would like to learn about such as details of a faculty member's research, what he or she looks for in a student, and opportunities available to students in the lab.

Perhaps the best way to prepare for interviews is to ask a friend, colleague, or current supervisor to conduct mock interviews. For applicants who are still affiliated with a college or university, it is worth exploring whether the school has an office or program (e.g., career development) that helps prepare students for interviews. Talk to friends who have been through the process. Although preparing for interviews can be difficult and there are many unknowns, a variety of resources, including practice questions, are readily available online.

Interview Format

Most programs require an in-person interview, but some may only offer remote interviews conducted via phone or Skype. At times, you will have a choice between the two. It is important to carefully weigh the pros and cons of each. On the one hand, you have the best shot of making a lasting impression in person; you can also gauge your feel for the program, a larger set of faculty and students, and the location, which may be your home for the next 4–6 years. Interview days are important for gathering data, and there is only so much that can be learned remotely for both the interviewer and interviewee. On the other hand, you can avoid a potential conflict with another program (e.g., conducting a Skype interview at the end of an in-person interview day elsewhere) and save a considerable amount of money. To maximize your chances of admission, it is important to prioritize attending in-person interviews for the programs that are highest on your list.

INTERVIEW DAY(S)

The day has finally arrived! Interview day can look different depending on the program, ranging from one interview with a faculty member to a full day of informational sessions, tours, and multiple interviews with faculty and current students. Although the latter is common for doctoral programs, most applicants will not get the full interview schedule until interview day.

Pre-/post-events

Many interviews for doctoral programs involve social events, such as dinners or cocktail hours, the night before or immediately following interview day. Sometimes, only current and prospective graduate students – not faculty – are invited to these events. These can be a great opportunity to display more of your personality and interests in a low(er)-stress environment. Attending these events likely will not make or break your application. If you have 24 hours to travel to another state for an interview, then it may not make sense for you to attend the social event. If, on the other hand, interview-related anxiety is generating avoidance, then you may want to don your social butterfly wings and tough it out for the day. These are usually more relaxed events, and while you still want to make a good impression, you can also have more natural conversations than on interview day itself. More on that later.

Social events for prospective students should be treated as part of the interview process. Although faculty members may not attend dinners or cocktail hours, which relieves some of the pressure for a few hours, encounters with current graduate students are often factored into the decision-making process when it comes time to extend offers of admission. Regardless of the setting, be punctual, prepared, professional, and dressed to impress (Hodge, 2013), and be friendly and respectful to everyone that you meet at these events.

The Main Event

Interviews can be conducted with faculty members and current graduate students either in a one-on-one or group setting. The most influential interview will be with the faculty member with whom you applied to work. It is safe to assume that you have reached this stage based on your impressive qualifications on paper. However, in doctoral programs, which are typically selective and small, prospective mentors also want to know if you are someone with whom they want to work closely for several years and subsequently guide into the field as a colleague.

Besides questions about your experiences, you should be prepared to discuss your interest in forensic psychology. You should also have a sense of your research interests, particularly if research is a central focus of the program. Additionally, you will likely be asked about your goals during graduate school and as a professional. Often, faculty members and current students will discuss ongoing or future research. Although you may have a specific interest, keep an open mind. Be receptive to different research projects and opportunities. It is likely that your interests will change or grow during graduate school. Creating the impression that you are not interested in other topics may be perceived as a sign of inflexibility.

In addition to gaining a sense of your fit with the program, interviewers consider how the program fits with your goals and interests. Be prepared to answer questions about the program's appeal to you. Although you have likely ranked or prioritized certain programs over others, there is no such thing as a "safety school" during the application process, and you should not treat any program as such during the interview. Demonstrate a strong interest in the program and gather information throughout the day. It is possible that a program you believed to be your dream school will disappoint you on interview day, while a program to which you applied on a whim (which, by the way, is not recommended) now seems like a perfect fit. Bear in mind the competitive nature of the process. Even if your scores and academic background exceed program averages, you are not guaranteed admission because other interviewees are likely also over-qualified.

Hodge (2013) suggests discussing several topics during an interview, including the prospective mentor's level of contact and communication with graduate students, expectations for lab members, structure of lab meetings, and opportunities for research, presentations, and publications. Recommended topics for other faculty or current graduate students include coursework expectations, schedules, and stipends (Hodge, 2013).

Asking thoughtful and unique questions is a great way to demonstrate your interest and personality. Also, although it is natural to feel like interviewing for such a coveted position is a gift, you want to think critically about whether this is a place in which you see yourself living and thriving for a number of years.

As much as possible, try to generate a discussion rather than following a question-and-answer interview structure (Oudekerk & Bottoms, 2007). This is a good way to demonstrate your curiosity, thinking processes, ability to engage in relevant academic conversation, and knowledge about the field. It is also a more interesting and engaging experience for your interviewer, who will be conducting multiple interviews over the course of the day. Throughout the interviews, it is important to provide a sense of you as a person. With all of the academic and professional preparation that goes into the graduate application process, it is not uncommon for applicants to freeze when asked about hobbies or interests – characteristics about yourself *beyond* your professional accomplishments.

Try to strike a balance between presenting your "true" self and being respectful of expected norms. Although part of this process is getting a feel for whether you will enjoy working together as colleagues and peers, you also want to communicate how you will operate in professional settings, such as conferences or forensic contexts, in addition to providing a sense of your personality.

You may be asked about other interviews, acceptances, or "top choice" programs, which can be uncomfortable to address. As with the standard "What is your greatest weakness?" interview question, be prepared to be diplomatic. Remember that even if you end up attending a different school, the field of forensic psychology is a small world and collaboration is common. It is not advisable to speak poorly about other programs because your interviewer may personally know the person about whom you are speaking, or to promise a faculty member you will accept an offer if you have no intention of doing so. If you characterize a program as your top choice and communicate that to the faculty member, there is an expectation you will accept an offer.

Ultimately, programs and faculty members approach the interview process differently. They may ask a lot of questions, present clinical or research questions for you to answer on the spot, primarily provide you with information about the program, or ultimately just want to get a sense of you as a person and what unique characteristics, abilities, and experiences you will bring to the table. Be open to and prepared for each possibility. Flexibility in the interview process is key.

Perhaps the biggest thing to remember is that it is natural to be nervous! The application and interview process are anxiety-provoking, and they require considerable time, energy, and effort to continuously put your best foot forward. Make time to prepare sufficiently while also engaging in self-care.

Post-interview

Sending thank you e-mails is a common courtesy after the interview. Although it is not necessarily a make-or-break decision, doing so is a good opportunity to express gratitude for the time and effort programs put into conducting interviews and to remind faculty and graduate students of shared interests. When possible, avoid a generic "thank you" e-mail and instead try to include something that stood out. For example, "I really enjoyed hearing about the research your lab is conducting, and it was interesting to learn that you are an avid runner." Including a personal observation like that can reflect your thoughtfulness and connection.

Sadly, what comes next is more waiting … It is not recommended to keep contacting programs or mentors after the interview, or to provide regular updates about your status as an applicant (Oudekerk & Bottoms, 2007). The exception is if you have accepted an offer from another program or you realize after the interview that you will definitely not accept an offer from the program; these things should be communicated to the relevant programs affected by your decision. Exercise patience during this process and take a well-deserved break to reward yourself for the hard work you have put in thus far.

THE FINAL VERDICT

Typically, doctoral programs inform applicants of their decision by April 1st at the latest, with a deadline for the applicant to accept or decline an offer of April 15th (Prinstein, 2017). It is possible that you will be notified at a later date if you are on a waitlist, but programs will usually inform applicants of waitlist status.

How to Decide

It can be nearly as hard as, if not harder than, the other stages of the application and interview process to decide among multiple offers. Having multiple offers is a great "problem" to have, but it complicates the decision-making process. It is important to carefully weigh the pros and cons of each program, including factors that may have felt irrelevant earlier on, such as location and longer-term considerations (e.g., clinical exposure to forensic populations). This is the stage at which it becomes particularly useful to have been a conscientious observer during interview days and to have noted the program's fit with your goals.

How to Say "No"

When deciding among schools, carefully consider your options while also being mindful of the other programs and waitlisted applicants. It might seem unbelievable to imagine that, after all this time, money, and anxiety, anyone would choose not to enroll in graduate school if offered the opportunity. However, it happens. This is not a nail in the coffin of your eventual career as a forensic psychologist. If you were competitive as an applicant one year, it is likely that you will continue to be competitive with even more research or clinical experience under your belt.

Once you make a decision, notify the programs as soon as possible. Remember that other applicants may be waiting for an offer from the same program, so holding on to the offer may prevent those applicants from getting the good news. Being respectful of the schools – and other applicants – is part of good professional conduct. When declining an offer, you may choose to e-mail or call the faculty members with whom you interviewed. Thank them for their time, reiterate that it was a difficult decision, and (if true) note that you look forward to seeing them in another professional context or potentially collaborating at some point. If you applied to forensic programs, the latter is a real possibility given the tight-knit academic/professional community.

SO IT DIDN'T WORK OUT …

Rejection does not feel good, and if it did not work out in your favor, then the graduate application process is a particularly protracted and mentally, emotionally, and financially burdensome route to dis- appointment. Take the time to lament the process, and then remind yourself that this is hard, selective, and competitive. Many applicants who are not successful one year can gain entry to graduate school in a subsequent year.

Being rejected from graduate school is not necessarily an indication that you are not qualified or not cut out to be a forensic psychologist. Certainly, some applicants are simply not qualified and may never become sufficiently qualified for graduate school, and the unfortunate reality is that those applicants may need to choose a different profession. However, given how competitive it is to gain admission to a doctoral program, many highly qualified applicants will not be accepted. The supply of potential graduate students far exceeds the available slots. Over- all, fewer than 10% of applicants to doctoral programs in clinical psychol- ogy are accepted, and the acceptance rate can be as low as 2–3% for more competitive programs (Stamm et al., 2016). Being invited to interview is a notable accomplishment and learning opportunity. Even if you were not invited to interview, the application process is still a learning opportunity. If becoming a forensic psychologist is truly your goal, then achieving that goal may involve tolerating setbacks and being flexible about your roadmap. It is unlikely you will be a *less* competitive applicant 1 year later, but you still want to maximize the likelihood of success in the future. Luckily, there are things you can do to improve your chances the next time around.

Alternative Acceptances

Although you might not be accepted into the program to which you applied, you may receive an alternative opportunity at the same institution. Some programs will offer doctoral applicants a spot in their master's program; some applications have a designation to indicate if you are interested in being considered for this option. Additionally, a lab or program may invite you to join the team in a research capacity as an employee or volunteer. This is a great opportunity to demonstrate your abilities and commitment, and to gain real-world experience and insight into the workings of a program in which you hope to be enrolled in the future.

Next Steps

Back to the drawing board. If you have decided to apply for graduate school during the next cycle, you might choose to expand your search to include programs or degree options you may not have considered originally. Additionally, the faculty who are admitting students for the subsequent application year will likely change, introducing fresh opportunities. It is also a good idea to stay professionally involved and continue to network by submitting to and attending conferences, enrolling in relevant workshops, and joining professional organizations.

QUESTIONS TO ASK YOURSELF IF APPLYING DID NOT WORK OUT THIS TIME AROUND

- Can my GRE scores be improved?
- Have I contributed to posters, publications, or research presentations?
- Is there a gap in my CV where I can gain research or clinical experience?
- Are there other opportunities to pursue aside from obtaining a doctoral degree?

It is important to critically evaluate your CV if you are not accepted into graduate school. Positive change and taking the initiative to strengthen your qualifications will be viewed favorably by admissions committees. You may find creative ways to build experience, such as volunteering at a crisis center to gain clinical experience or conducting independent research under a current mentor or supervisor. If you have just graduated college, select your post-college job carefully with these factors in mind. Chances are, your future graduate student self will appreciate the financial cushion from a few years' worth of salary, not to mention that real-world experience is invaluable and will equip you with useful skills to highlight in later applications.

Another domain that calls for critical evaluation is "fit." Reevaluate your training and career goals in comparison to the programs and faculty members to whom you applied. It can be easy to conflate a vague or fleeting interest with true enthusiasm or intent. It can also be easy to set your sights on a renowned school or faculty member. In many ways, fit is more important than name at the graduate level (Fowler, 2016). The process of obtaining a doctoral degree is highly individualized, and programs want to invest in students for whom they can help build a meaningful career.

If the graduate application process was not successful the first time around, you do not have to give up on the goal of becoming a forensic psychologist. However, you should not expect vastly different outcomes if little changes between one application cycle and the next. Use this time to rest and relax before thinking carefully about how you can mold yourself into a stronger applicant and improve your chances of future admission.

★ ★ ★

CONCLUSION

It is normal to feel anxious about the application and interview process. Chances are, you may have felt nervous at various points throughout this chapter. Nothing about the application process is simple, fast, or inexpensive. But if you want a career in forensic psychology, the application process is important and obviously unavoidable.

Hopefully, throughout this chapter, we provided you with enough of a preliminary idea of what to expect and how to prepare for the application and interview process for doctoral programs. Assuming you made it through this chapter without throwing the book away and permanently hiding under a blanket, you may feel less anxious and better equipped to handle the challenges of applying and interviewing. Or you may be feeling more overwhelmed by what lies ahead. This is all normal! Remember, you are not alone in this process. You can reach out to colleagues, peers, supervisors, and knowledgeable strangers who have shared insights online. Being organized and planning ahead is key, but this *is* doable.

The Main Takeaways

- Start early and equip yourself with the tools to maximize your chances of success during the application and interview process.
- The primary components of most doctoral and many master's program applications are background information; a CV outlining relevant research, academic, and clinical experience; test scores; official transcripts; letters of recommendation; and a personal statement.
- Effectively budget your time, money, and resources – including those who have agreed to write letters of recommendation, proofread essays, and conduct mock interviews.
- Avoid (un)common missteps and "kisses of death."
- Prepare for your interviews by doing research, generating questions, conducting mock interviews, and addressing logistics to ease anxiety on interview day.
- If you are accepted into graduate school, weigh your options. If things did not work out as planned this time around, return to the drawing board to develop a targeted plan for improving your chances of success the next time around.
- Practice self-care. Remember, this is a necessary but extremely challenging and arduous process.

NOTES

1 For those interested in pursuing other degrees, additional resources may be found in Further Reading or on relevant graduate program websites.
2 It is typical to receive a formal report of your GRE test score approximately 10–15 days after test day if you completed the computer-administered version or 5 weeks after test day if you took the paper version (ETS, n.d.). Immediately upon completion of the computerized version, test takers can receive *unofficial* test scores for the Quantitative Reasoning and Verbal Reasoning sections, but graduate programs typically require official reports when submitting an application.

REFERENCES

American Psychological Association. (n.d.). *PSYCAS resources for students.* Retrieved from www.apa.org/education/grad/psycas-students.aspx
Appleby, D. C., & Appleby, K. M. (2006). Kisses of death in the graduate school application process. *Teaching of Psychology, 33*, 19–24.

Buffardi, L. E. (2014, October). Emailing future Ph.D. advisors. *Psychology Today.* Retrieved on July 20, 2019 from www.psychologytoday.com/us/blog/grad-school-guru/201410/emailing-future-phd-advisors

Clark, J. C. (2009, November). Rockin' recommendations: How to make sure you get the recommendation letters you deserve. *GradPSYCH Magazine.* Retrieved on July 20, 2019 from www.apa.org/gradpsych/features/2009/recommendation.aspx

ETS. (n.d.). *Frequently asked questions about the GRE® General Test.* Retrieved from www.ets.org/gre/revised_general/faq/

Fowler, G. A. (2016, June). Didn't get into graduate school? Here is your plan B. *APA Psych Learning Curve.* Retrieved on July 20, 2019 from http://psychlear ningcurve.org/plan-b/

Geher, G. (2017, November). Guidance on the graduate school application process: The do's and dont's of applying to graduate school for psych-related programs. *Psychology Today.* Retrieved on July 20, 2019 from www.psychologytoday.com/us/blog/darwins-subterranean-world/201711/guidance-the-graduate-school-application-process

Hayes, L. J., & Hayes, S. C. (1989, September). How to apply to graduate school. *APS Observer.*

Hodge, J. J. (2013, Summer). I have an interview! Now what? Demystifying the graduate school interview process. *APSSC Undergraduate Update.* Retrieved on July 20, 2019 from www.psychologicalscience.org/members/apssc/undergra duate_update/undergraduate-update-summer-2013/i-have-an-interview-now-what-demystifying-the-graduate-school-interview-process

Hogan, T. P. (2016). Preparing your personal statement for graduate school applications. *Psychology Student Network, 4,* 2.

Oudekerk, B. A., & Bottoms, B. L. (2007). Applying to graduate school: The interview process. *APS Observer, 20*(6). Retrieved on July 20, 2019 from www.psychologicalscience.org/observer/applying-to-graduate-school-the-inter view-process

Prinstein, M. J. (2017). Mitch's uncensored advice for applying to graduate school in clinical psychology. Retrieved on July 20, 2019 from http://mitch.web.unc.edu/files/2017/02/MitchGradSchoolAdvice.pdf

Stamm, K., Michalski, D., Cope, C., Fowler, G., Christidis, P., & Lin, L. (2016, February). Datapoint: What are the acceptance rates for graduate psychology programs? *Monitor on Psychology, 47*(2), 16.

CHAPTER 6

Hallowed Halls

Surviving and Thriving in Graduate School

Congratulations! Following a competitive application, interview, and decision-making process, you have finally arrived at your chosen graduate program to begin building your career as a forensic psychologist. Graduate school is a critical period for academic and professional development, and your pursuits as a student will set the stage for your career. Being a doctoral student requires that you wear many hats – student, clinician, and researcher, among others. Alongside the many exciting and formative opportunities that will be available to you, certain aspects of graduate school will be challenging, time consuming, and demanding.

As you gear up to begin graduate school, it is important to consider the skillset you hope to obtain and the career you wish to build for yourself. Although 5–7 years in a PhD program may sound – and at times feel – like a long time, there is a lot to accomplish in graduate school, and it likely will not be possible to commit to everything you want to do or are offered. Therefore, having goals and target experiences in mind can serve as a roadmap that guides how you choose to spend your time and energy during graduate school.

A clinical PhD program is a crucial step toward molding your career in preparation for formally entering the field of forensic psychology. These years provide rich opportunities to strengthen and distinguish yourself as a future job applicant. The research and clinical opportunities you pursue over time create a narrative – a story of your interests, background, and training – that lends itself to career prospects. To obtain your clinical doctoral degree, you need to survive graduate school, but to build your dream house – your ideal career as a forensic psychologist – you must also thrive.

This chapter provides an overview of clinical PhD programs, including universal requirements and additional opportunities, and discusses strategies that will help you not only make it through graduate school but also excel along the way. Although the process of pursuing other types of graduate degrees operates differently, the information covered in this chapter may be useful across a variety of graduate experiences and at many stages of the training process. Furthermore, regardless of whether your program has a specific forensic focus, there are likely several opportunities for relevant experience and training.

CLINICAL PHD PROGRAMS

What does a clinical doctoral program entail anyway? Clinical PhD programs are unique in their balance of three areas – research, clinical, and coursework – with varying emphasis on each depending on the program's orientation and training goals. Regardless of its relevance to the career you intend to develop, you will be expected to contribute time and effort to each component. Some programs also require students to successfully complete qualifying exams midway through graduate school or serve as a teaching assistant (TA) for undergraduate courses. All of which is to say that a lot is expected of graduate students. Fortunately, there are ways to maximize productivity and successfully manage all three realms.

THE RESEARCH REALM

Research may factor heavily into a career as a forensic psychologist. By conducting research, psychologists investigate important questions in the field, further examine existing phenomena, generate novel ideas, and evaluate interventions and procedures with the goal of impacting policy and practice. Regardless of whether you intend to pursue a research-based career, research is a necessary component of obtaining a PhD, and the skills required to conduct research are important for clinical work and the critical examination of laws/policy.

Research involvement, which typically begins during the first year of graduate school, is an opportunity to explore and narrow down your interests. In mentor-based programs, students may be expected to contribute to ongoing projects in a research lab. Also, students may take the initiative to get involved in research by assisting others in their labs or department with ongoing studies or collaborating with a mentor's colleagues remotely. Doing so is a good opportunity to identify potential research interests for future self-directed projects (e.g., dissertation).

Many clinical doctoral programs require completion of both a thesis and dissertation. Both projects provide the opportunity to examine the literature to generate a unique hypothesis, design a study, analyze data, and draw conclusions. This research is often presented in the form of both a written report and oral defense in front of a committee. Students who have one research topic they would like to explore may benefit from using the thesis as a precursor to a larger-scale or more comprehensive dissertation.

A **thesis** is typically a smaller-scale project completed midway through a doctoral program as a requirement for obtaining a master's degree.

A **dissertation**, the final step toward obtaining a doctoral degree, is one of the major highlights of a doctoral program and often requires more resources to complete than a thesis.

Types of Research

Forensic psychology research centers on the intersection between law and psychology. A wide variety of research topics can be pursued within the field, including factors that influence jury decision-making, the effectiveness of corrections or community-based interventions for justice-involved individuals, and the impact of training and psychoeducation on law enforcement, corrections, and legal professionals, among many others. Research can involve direct contact with research participants, analysis of existing data, or interviews and behavioral observations. Projects can be developed and implemented in a variety of ways. Therefore, even if research is not your primary passion or the reason you enrolled in graduate school, you will likely be able to generate a topic of interest to pursue.

Clinical Research Projects

Clinical forensic research, which largely focuses on justice-involved populations, may examine the use of assessments or interventions, or focus on the observation of phenomena related to psychological or behavioral disorders. Intervention-based research typically consists of developing and implementing treatment programs, or studying existing treatment programs, to examine outcomes such as risk reduction or improved psychological functioning. Many routes can be pursued within this larger framework. Examples include piloting a novel therapeutic intervention, applying an existing treatment to a select population (e.g., female sex offenders), examining outcomes for certain characteristics of interest (e.g., violence risk reduction), or comparing types of therapy (e.g., cognitive-behavioral therapy vs. acceptance and commitment therapy) to examine which is more effective for the population.

Forensic mental health assessment (i.e., the assessment of justice-involved individuals for the purpose of assisting legal decision-makers; see Chapter 2) is another major area of clinical research in forensic psychology (Heilbrun, Rogers, & Otto, 2002). Research questions may examine whether an assessment captures the phenomenon it intends to capture (e.g., whether a risk assessment measure accurately identifies high-risk offenders), how assessment serves to guide treatment (e.g., whether inmates receiving treatment tailored to their risk level demonstrate better outcomes than those assigned to treatment at random), or the utility of a newly developed assessment (e.g., whether a risk assessment measure is useful across age and gender).

An important consideration when conducting research or generating potential research ideas is the feasibility of the project. Graduate students often have limited time and resources to conduct research, and developing a novel intervention or gaining access to justice-involved populations can be challenging. One way to offset these barriers is to conduct a secondary analysis (i.e., analysis of existing data to answer a new research question). For example, a secondary analysis may examine whether an intervention that was developed to reduce violence risk also has an impact on overall psychological well-being. Using existing data saves both time and money, while simultaneously potentially addressing important forensic questions.

Public Perception and Policy-Based Research

Forensic-focused research sheds light on legal processes, such as the influence of juror characteristics on guilty verdicts or factors that influence sentencing. This research enhances the field's understanding of the justice process and can lead to recommendations to improve the legal system. These types of studies vary in complexity, ranging from easy-to-administer surveys to challenging experimental studies.

Non-clinical research can also examine public perception to gain a sense of society's opinion on or awareness of certain justice-related concepts, with the goal of impacting policy or practice. Some examples include perceptions of the death penalty, solitary confinement, or police tactics. The general population can also be surveyed as a proxy for jurors. This type of research also allows for the examination of common misconceptions in the field, the results of which can potentially be used to improve the administration of justice.

FORENSIC FUN FACT

Faulty eyewitness testimony and false confessions are two of the most common reasons for wrongful convictions in the United States. Forensic psychological research has been essential in shedding light on the mechanisms underlying these phenomena.

Additional Forms of Research

Students may conduct research with general populations to examine forensic phenomena (e.g., eyewitness identification, false confessions); this approach can be particularly useful due to the challenges associated with gaining access to justice-involved populations of criminal offenders. Students can also conduct in-depth, comprehensive reviews of the research published on certain topics to obtain a more complete understanding of what we know in that area. These types of studies, often called meta-analyses or systematic reviews, provide both the "big picture" of all of the research conducted on a particular topic and a more detailed look at what we actually know about the topic. For example, a researcher might review all of the research conducted on jail-based therapy with violent offenders to gain a more complete understanding of the types of treatment that are provided and the effectiveness of those interventions in reducing risk.

How to Proceed

Now that you have a sense of what conducting research projects as a graduate student entails, you might be wondering how and where to start.

WHAT TO CONSIDER WHEN CONDUCTING RESEARCH IN GRADUATE SCHOOL

- Identify existing sources of data
- Create opportunities for data gathering
- Collaborate with peers and colleagues
- Apply for funding and financial support
- Seek continuing education opportunities

Identifying Sources of Data versus Creating Opportunities

There are many sources of existing data that are waiting to be analyzed. Securing existing data allows students to sidestep data collection, saving significant time and resources. Potential sources may include publicly available datasets, previous projects conducted by a research mentor, or government entities (e.g., Departments of Corrections) that regularly collect data but may not always conduct in-depth analyses. This route may prove particularly fruitful for smaller-scale side projects conducted throughout graduate school.

That being said, there is significant value in developing a research project from the ground up, including designing a study, collecting data, and analyzing data. Approaching a mentor or faculty member with a unique research idea may set you apart from other students and provide an opportunity to take the lead on a project. Also, designing a study allows you to examine a specific research question in the format of your choosing. This process provides valuable firsthand experience with the many decision points and challenges associated with research.

Collaboration

As will be emphasized throughout this chapter, collaboration is a critical component of graduate school success. Within the realm of research, collaboration provides greater latitude of areas of study and helps to facilitate the completion of a project. On a smaller scale, research collaboration can take place across labs, departments, or programs. Because forensic psychology is inherently cross-disciplinary, a benefit is that research collaboration can occur across disciplines. Subfields of psychology (e.g., neuropsychology) can be readily applied to the legal system, and different fields (e.g., legal, correctional) overlap significantly with forensic psychology. The growth of the field of forensic psychology allows for networking and collaboration on an (inter)national level, which is a great way to expand one's scope of work and gain access to interesting opportunities and populations.

Funding and Support

Another consideration throughout graduate school that is particularly relevant to conducting research is financial support. Depending on the scope of the study, financial support may be necessary to compensate participants, purchase study materials, and pay research assistants, among other costs.

Various sources and types of funding exist to support graduate research projects, including funding awarded for the development of a thesis or dissertation project or travel awards to attend conferences and disseminate research findings. Although some awarding entities use the terms interchangeably, grants are typically provided to graduate students to support the cost of conducting the research, whereas fellowships may also be used to offset tuition or provide money that goes directly to the student. Fellowships may also provide access to academic resources, training, and networking opportunities. In addition to presenting an excellent opportunity to obtain funding, familiarity with the grant application process is a valuable skill and helps to build your curriculum vitae (CV) – both of which will strengthen your status as a future applicant to internship or for a research or academic job.

Funding may be available from a variety of sources, including your graduate program or institution, state-based psychological organizations (e.g., Pennsylvania Psychological Association), federal organizations (e.g., National Institutes of Health), the American Psychological Association (APA) or American Psychological Association of Graduate Students (APAGS), American Psychological Foundation (APF), American Psychology-Law Society (AP-LS; Division 41 of APA), the American Academy of Forensic Psychology (AAFP), and Psi Chi (international honor society for psychology) (Novotney, 2011). Organizations run by the federal government, including the National Institutes of Health and National Science Foundation, offer highly prestigious and competitive funding opportunities for graduate students.[1] Private foundations can also serve as a source of research funding, including the International Dissertation Research Fellowship Program provided by the Andrew W. Mellon Foundation, which is awarded to full-time graduate students conducting research internationally, and the Harry Frank Guggenheim Foundation's Dissertation Fellowships, which are awarded to researchers who investigate violence and aggression related to social change, intergroup conflict, crime, and family relationships (Novotney, 2011).

Graduate funding opportunities may be general (e.g., to support clinical psychology dissertations), related to forensic psychology (e.g., focused on diversity research), or forensic-specific (e.g., research conducted on violence risk). Although several sources of funding are available, the process of obtaining a grant or fellowship is competitive, so applying for a wide variety of both large and small grants is advisable. For those who plan to conduct an ambitious project that may require several years to complete (e.g., developing and piloting a novel intervention for incarcerated youth), obtaining research funding may be particularly appealing.

Continuing Education

Students who intend to pursue a research-focused career may choose to further their education or strengthen their familiarity with certain aspects of the research process. This can be achieved by enrolling in advanced statistics and research methods courses or by attending relevant workshops.

In sum, contributing to existing research and conducting your own research are necessary for success in most doctoral programs, many of which involve completing both a thesis and dissertation project at a minimum. To survive, you should be aware of the different types of research and begin to identify possible research interests. To thrive, you should collaborate, diversify, and aim to do more than what is required by your program. Collaborate and offer to help others with research, initiate your own projects if a specific research question appeals to you, and seek sources of funding through grants or fellowships. Additionally, you can maximize the impact of your research projects by disseminating your research findings in publications and conference presentations; we discuss dissemination of research later in this chapter.

THE CLINICAL REALM

When some people think of forensic psychology, the first thing that comes to mind may not be therapy, but clinical work plays a significant role in the field and it is important to develop clinical skills. Forensic psychologists often conduct evaluations of defendants to address questions such as whether the defendant is competent to stand trial or to identify whether the defendant has specific characteristics (e.g., low IQ level or psychiatric symptoms) that may be relevant to sentencing. These tasks require training in clinical interviewing, conducting and interpreting psychological testing, and report writing. Forensic psychologists may also conduct therapy with offenders during or following a period of incarceration. Finally, clinical training in graduate school is a prerequisite for future licensure and board certification (for a more in-depth discussion, see Chapter 9).

Practicum training experiences are field experiences through which graduate students receive supervised training as clinicians (APA, 2006). Practicum placements are typically 1-year placements consisting of part-time work (10–16 hours per week) at local training facilities.

Regardless of how it factors into your long-term career goals, clinical training and education comprise another critical and required component of pursuing a clinical PhD on the road to becoming a forensic psychologist. For doctoral programs to be APA-accredited, graduate students must complete practicum training. Approximately 70% of clinical and counseling psychology programs have students begin clinical training during their second year, while 30% begin during their first year (Hatcher, Wise, & Grus, 2015). Through these experiences, students receive training in real-world settings that allow for direct patient contact through providing therapy, conducting assessments, developing case conceptualizations and treatment plans, and receiving supervision from licensed clinicians. Additionally, these placements pave the road to securing an internship (i.e., a full-time clinical placement that typically serves as the last year of doctoral training), which is a requirement of most clinical doctoral programs and a highly competitive process (see Chapter 7).

For many, graduate school will be the first foray into clinical work and perhaps the first foray into working directly with justice-involved populations. It is common to be nervous about clinical training, and this anxiety will likely continue to emerge at various points in your training. However, by equipping yourself with knowledge about these opportunities and identifying what you hope to obtain from your graduate clinical training, you can set yourself up for success.

Types of Clinical Work

Broadly speaking, clinical work involves providing services to individuals, couples, or families to address a variety of behavioral and mental health concerns. It can consist of both assessment (i.e., testing and forming diagnoses) and intervention (i.e., providing psychotherapy to populations in an individual or group setting) (APA, n.d.a). Within this broad definition, there is considerable variability, and clinical experiences may differ depending on the population, theoretical orientation (e.g., behavioral, psychodynamic), and treatment provider.

Assessment versus Therapy

Assessment and evaluations are typically conducted for the purpose of diagnosing a patient and forming a treatment plan. This approach often consists of a clinical interview covering psychosocial domains (e.g., family background, social history, mental health symptoms) and psychological or cognitive/intellectual testing (Framingham, 2016). As noted in Chapter 1, forensic assessment is conducted to address a legal question as opposed to a clinical one, whereas interventions or psychotherapy involve the provision of ongoing treatment to address a patient's mental health needs.

Forensic Psychology versus Correctional Psychology

To strengthen your prospects as a future forensic psychologist, it is important to obtain clinical experience in both assessment and therapy, which maps on to forensic psychology and correctional psychology, respectively. Forensic psychology involves forming opinions about criminal offenders or civil litigants when there is a legal issue for which psychological expertise is useful (Neal, 2018). This often occurs pre-adjudication (i.e., prior to a determination of guilt), as with evaluations of competence to stand trial (see Chapter 2). In contrast, correctional psychology involves the application of psychology in jail, prison, or another correctional or community setting specifically for the classification, treatment, and management of offenders (Neal, 2018). This approach involves providing an intervention or ongoing treatment and typically occurs post-adjudication (i.e., after a finding of guilt). For example, inmates may receive group therapy in prison, or individuals may be referred to therapy upon supervised release (e.g., parole) to address existing psychological symptoms and challenges associated with reentering society.

Types of Clinical Settings

Clinical work can take place in a variety of contexts, and you will likely have access to different options as a graduate student. Each option can be general or specific in terms of the types of services provided (e.g., neuropsychological testing), the format (e.g., individual, group, couples, teletherapy), and population (e.g., children, justice-involved adults). On a basic level, practicum placements can be in either an inpatient or outpatient setting.

Inpatient Settings

In inpatient settings, clinicians work with individuals residing in a treatment facility for a period of time, ranging from a short hospital stay to months or years, on either a voluntary or involuntary basis. These settings include residential treatment facilities, corrections-based treatment centers, and hospital psychiatric units. Inpatient treatment provides the opportunity for collaboration with a range of treatment providers (e.g., physicians, social workers), and the populations in these facilities may exhibit more severe forms of mental illness.

Outpatient Settings

Practicum placements can also be community-based. Outpatient mental health clinics may be in a variety of settings, including an independent or university-based clinic. University-based clinics are often training clinics that serve the community at large or college students specifically. Intensive outpatient clinics are sometimes located in or affiliated with hospitals, affording the same benefits of access to interdisciplinary training. Outpatient practica can also take place in a private practice, which is run independently by an individual or small group and typically has a specific focus or specialty (e.g., treating anxiety disorders).

Forensic-specific Settings

Additional settings specific to forensic psychology include jails, prisons, state/forensic hospitals, courthouses or legal offices, private practices for forensic psychologists, and residential treatment facilities for justice-involved populations. Forensic patients may be court-mandated to receive treatment or be evaluated based on a court order or at the request of their attorney. Therefore, working closely with courts, lawyers, transitional housing services, and corrections staff is a common part of clinical forensic training.

How to Proceed

Now that you are familiar with the types of clinical training opportunities that may be available to you during practicum placements, you may be wondering how to make the right choices or how to seek certain opportunities.

WHAT TO CONSIDER WHEN OBTAINING CLINICAL EXPERIENCE IN GRADUATE SCHOOL

- Plan ahead
- Check boxes by meeting APPIC requirements for internship applications
- Identify clinical forensic opportunities
- Diversify your training experiences
- Put your best foot forward by fostering strong, professional relationships
- Specialize at the practicum level by working with populations or interventions of interest
- Seek continuing education opportunities

Planning Ahead

A foundational key to success is to identify the opportunities you want to pursue and plan accordingly. In addition to working in specific settings or with specific populations, it is important to obtain varied experience to build core competencies, including assessment and intervention skills, knowledge of evidence-based practices, and familiarity with ethical standards (Voelker, 2015). Due to the limited number of years available for practicum, securing a sufficient range of opportunities requires advanced planning. It is beneficial to express these desired training goals to mentors or others in your program who can provide insight into relevant clinical sites. Graduate students undergo the same process yearly, so you have access to people who can speak to the pros and cons of a certain training experience.

The Association of Psychology Postdoctoral and Internship Centers (APPIC), which is the centralized organization for internship applications and placement, collects annual data on the average qualifications of applicants. For the 2017 application year, the median hours reported by applicants was 598 intervention hours and 178 assessment hours, and applicants reported a median of eight adult integrated reports and six child integrated reports (Keilin, 2018).

Checking Boxes

Internship sites have expectations for applicants that should be factored into practicum training to increase the likelihood of securing an internship (for an in-depth discussion, see Chapter 7). Expectations differ, but most internships require a mix of intervention and assessment hours and experience writing integrated reports (APPIC, n.d.).[2] Some students will know in advance to which sites they hope to apply and thus can gather the necessary information to secure their practicum placements accordingly. For students who do not have a specific plan for internship, obtaining a range of experiences can be advantageous. For forensic internships, graduate students should strive to attain training in conducting forensic assessments, report writing, and evidence-based interventions with forensic populations.

Identifying Clinical Forensic Opportunities

Many clinical doctoral programs offer community-based clinical opportunities that are affiliated with the school. For students in a program with a forensic focus, the program may offer forensic training opportunities through internal clinics or faculty members' private practices. Otherwise, students may have to pursue or create forensic practica opportunities by contacting potential supervisors in the community or, in select cases, by contributing to the development of an intervention to treat a forensic population of interest.[3] Nonetheless, if direct access to forensic populations is not available, then students can pursue opportunities that are similar in treatment target (e.g., aggression, serious mental illness), format (e.g., group therapy), or population (e.g., underserved).

Diversifying Experiences

Graduate students interested in a career in forensic psychology may also pursue general practicum opportunities (e.g., outpatient community mental health center) or choose to focus on a specific age group (e.g., adolescents), diagnosis (e.g., post-traumatic stress disorder), or subpopulation (e.g., veterans). The decision to pursue solely forensic versus a wide breadth of training opportunities depends in large part on your goals for internship and your career. For example, it may prove advantageous to diversify clinical experiences to gain well-rounded training and acquire skills appropriate for more general internship opportunities (e.g., a hospital setting with a forensic rotation).

Putting Your Best Foot Forward

If you hope to pursue or integrate clinical work into your career, then it is important to make the most of your practicum experiences in graduate school. Building strong, professional relationships with supervisors and colleagues and seeking feedback throughout your training is important because these individuals can serve as references for internship and future jobs (Voelker, 2015). Additionally, setting goals, including identifying what you hope to obtain from specific practicum placements and expressing these intentions to supervisors, will increase your likelihood of obtaining the experience and training you want (Voelker, 2015). Importantly, if clinical work is a major focus during your time in graduate school, seek opportunities beyond what is expected of you, including conducting research within a clinic, becoming a peer supervisor, assisting with the development of an intervention, and generating publications based on your experience.

Specializing at the Practicum Level

Although it is important for students interested in forensic psychology to gain forensic experience, pursuing narrow training opportunities may decrease your chances of being competitive for internships. For example, if a student narrowly focused his or her experience during graduate school on working with offenders, gaining an internship at a college counseling center may be challenging. Importantly, as with much of graduate school, practicum placements are an ideal opportunity for exploration of interests, so if you think you might enjoy a certain clinical experience (e.g., treating post-traumatic stress disorder at a local Veterans Affairs hospital), then pursuing a related practicum is beneficial.

Continuing Education

Many trainings and workshops are offered to teach clinicians and those in training specific types of therapy or how to effectively address clinical concerns (e.g., suicidality). These may be offered through a graduate program or in the community. Webinars facilitate widespread access to training. In addition to providing an opportunity to familiarize yourself with a variety of theoretical orientations, populations, diagnoses, and types of therapy, workshops and trainings allow for professional networking.

Regardless of your goals, clinical work is a critical component of pursuing a career in forensic psychology. To survive, you must obtain clinical training through practicum placements and courses to gain assessment and therapy experience. It is also necessary to obtain "support" experience through supervision, scoring/interpreting psychological tests, and writing clinical notes and reports. To thrive, you should identify varied experiences that increase your chances of becoming a competitive future internship applicant who has well-rounded experience with diverse populations in multiple settings. Additionally, work to build good relationships with supervisors and colleagues and to bridge areas of interest. Do more than what is expected of you, and seek the opportunities you wish to obtain, including working with specific populations, developing or evaluating treatments, and pursuing additional training in areas of interest.

THE ACADEMIC REALM

The final core component of a clinical doctoral program is coursework. All APA-accredited programs must include a curriculum that incorporates research methods; history and development of systems of psychology; data analysis; social, biological, and cognitive-affective aspects of behavior; ethics; psychopathology; human development; interventions, including theories and evaluation; consultation and supervision; and culture and diversity (APA, 2006). Programs with major areas of study (formerly known as concentrations) will likely have additional, concentration-specific course requirements. For students in forensic programs, course-work is a good opportunity to gain knowledge about the field (Burl, Shah, Filone, Foster, & DeMatteo, 2012; DeMatteo, Marczyk, Krauss, & Burl, 2009). For students in a more general program, certain coursework (e.g., intelligence testing, personality assessment, multicultural considerations) will still be applicable to forensic psychology. Additionally, opportunities may exist to complete coursework in other departments, such as criminology or law.

The emphasis on coursework relative to other responsibilities varies by program, and despite competing priorities and demands, students must perform well in their courses. On a practical level, much of the coursework doctoral students must complete lends itself to the research and clinical work that will be expected of you as a student, including statistics, intervention and assessment, ethical considerations for conducting research and therapy, and manuscript preparation. Additionally, graduate grade point averages are reported to internship sites during the application process. Therefore, graduate school is not a time to slack off on academics.

Qualifying (Comprehensive) Exams

Many doctoral programs require students to successfully pass a qualifying or comprehensive exam midway through the program to gauge student progress. The structure and content of qualifying exams vary across programs, but what you have learned in your courses will be particularly useful. The exam can be written, oral, or some combination of both, and it can follow a traditional exam format (e.g., multiple-choice and short-answer questions) or be practical in nature, such as providing a clinical presentation or developing a research proposal. Qualifying exams are often

To prepare for doctoral qualifying (comprehensive exams), Dingfelder (2004) suggests generating reading lists, being aware of recent changes to the field, consolidating notes from courses, organizing study materials and resources in advance, and seeking advice from other students.

viewed with apprehension by students, but many students have been through similar processes and are willing to share valuable insight and strategies.

How to Proceed

It can be difficult to imagine taking a full course load as a doctoral student on top of clinical and research expectations. Although courses are a necessary component of graduate school, there are ways that you can capitalize on time spent in this realm.

WHAT TO CONSIDER WHEN COMPLETING COURSEWORK IN GRADUATE SCHOOL

- Maximize on the requirements by overlapping projects and goals
- Pick coursework carefully
- Attend seminars and join webinars for additional didactics beyond classes

---

Maximize on the Requirements

Maximize your productivity by creatively identifying ways in which a course requirement may translate to other "to-dos." For example, you might write a research paper for a course that can be submitted for publication, or perhaps analyze your own research data for relevant course projects.

Pick Coursework Carefully (As Much as Possible)

Although core coursework is determined by APA for accreditation purposes, it is likely possible to enroll in specific classes (e.g., mental health law, forensic assessment) that are relevant to your research or clinical training. Additionally, courses present a great opportunity to obtain exposure to certain topics with which you would not otherwise be familiar (e.g., neuroanatomy).

Attend Seminars and Join Webinars

If you are interested in a specific topic that is not available through your coursework, clinical, or research opportunities, consider attending a seminar. Advancements in technology and cross-collaboration facilitate access to additional instruction through webinars. These can be a great source of furthering education, inspiration, and collaboration. Several organizations, including the AP-LS, American Academy of Forensic Psychology, and Consolidated Continuing Education and Professional Training, provide training seminars and/or webinars on forensic psychology topics.

To survive in the academic realm of graduate school, you must complete certain coursework requirements and maintain good academic standing. Successful completion of qualifying or comprehensive exams is also key for some programs. However, to thrive, think about how to maximize on the utility of your coursework. Generate publications, collaborate with others, and seek opportunities to learn about topics that may be useful to you in the future.

BEYOND THE BASICS

By now, we have covered the fundamentals of graduate school in clinical psychology – research, clinical, and academic – including what will be expected of you and how to excel beyond basic requirements. Although the necessary components may already have you wondering how you can possibly accomplish everything in just a few years, there are many more opportunities that can help foster a meaningful, successful career. These years are the building blocks of your future dream house, which should be laid carefully and successfully.

PUBLICATIONS

Publishing is a primary route for disseminating research findings and theoretical considerations in forensic psychology. The emphasis on publishing in graduate school varies across labs and programs. Although publishing articles is not a requirement for graduate school, doing so allows you to foster professional development, hone your academic writing skills, and build your CV.

A common maxim among those in academic positions is **"Publish or perish,"** meaning that publishing is necessary to build and sustain one's career as an academic or research psychologist.

Types of Publications

Journal Articles

How and what you publish can look different throughout your graduate career. The most common approach for psychologists is to publish journal articles, which are often empirical (i.e., presenting results of a research study) and relatively short; APA suggests that manuscripts should not exceed 35 double-spaced pages (APA, 2010). In addition to publishing original research, journal articles may be meta-analyses, literature reviews, case studies, theoretical reviews, and occasionally commentaries on other articles.

The peer-review process is considered the "gold standard" for selecting manuscripts for publication in an academic journal, and the publication of a peer-reviewed article indicates that the "quality and potential contribution of a manuscript has been evaluated by one's peers in the science community" (APA, n.d.b). This process is conducted impartially and is usually blinded (i.e., neither the author nor reviewers are aware of the other's identity), with the goal of ensuring responsible research and publishing. The top-tier journals are highly competitive, with manuscript rejection rates of over 80%. Getting an article published in any of these journals signals a marked contribution to the field.

> Common forensic psychology peer-reviewed journals include *Behavioral Sciences and the Law*, *Criminal Justice and Behavior*, *Law and Human Behavior*, and *Psychology, Public Policy, and Law* (see Chapter 2 for more information on forensic psychology journals).

Book Chapters or Books

Book chapters, or contributions to an edited book, are invited publications, which means that the book editor will solicit chapters on certain topics from identified professionals. Chapter authors are selected based on their expertise and reputation, and it is considered an honor to be invited to write a book chapter. It is rare for graduate students to be invited to write a chapter by a book editor, but graduate students can potentially co-author a book chapter being written by their mentor or supervisor. A benefit of writing a chapter is that it is virtually guaranteed to be published because it is an invited submission, assuming the chapter is submitted on time and addresses the agreed-upon topic.

It is also possible to contribute to a book as a graduate student, although such opportunities are far rarer early in one's career. Books can either come to fruition similarly to book chapters, whereby a publisher approaches a prospective author with a particular vision or topic in mind, or alternatively through the development of a book proposal that is shopped around to various publishers. Although it is highly unlikely that you will be approached directly as a graduate student to write a book, your mentor or supervisor may be approached to write a book. Therefore, expressing your goals in terms of academic writing early on in graduate school may increase the likelihood of being considered for such opportunities when they arise.

Law Reviews

A less-common publication outlet for doctoral students is law reviews, which are journals typically edited and published by a committee of law students, although they may also be affiliated with an organization. Law reviews may be of particular interest for those whose research maps on to legal policy or for those seeking to reach a legal audience. Publishing in law reviews is relatively uncommon for forensic professionals. Additionally, a few law reviews are particularly specialized to showcase articles related to mental and behavioral health.

Miscellaneous Writing Opportunities

Additional writing opportunities have become available in recent years, particularly for those who are adept at or interested in gaining experience with broader styles of writing. For example, students can potentially contribute to a column (i.e., a recurring piece based on a theme), such as the APA *Monitor*'s Judicial Notebook, which addresses novel legal issues (e.g., gun ownership rights for those with suspected mental illness) or Supreme Court cases (e.g., *Miller* v. *Alabama*, 2012) relevant to forensic psychology. The APA *Monitor* is the official magazine of APA, and it is published 11 times per year and received by over 100,000 APA members. Additionally, some journals publish abstracts (or short summaries) of conference presentations, which provides an opportunity for a student to add a presentation and publication (on the same topics) to his or her CV. Blogs and websites provide a unique opportunity for more general and creative writing because they allow for non-empirical content (e.g., commentary, advice for graduate students). Finally, APA's *gradPSYCH*, which is published as part of the APA *Monitor* and focuses on graduate student concerns (e.g., internship interviews, securing funding), offers an opportunity for graduate students to publish articles.

How to Proceed

Regardless of the medium, academic writing – and writing in general – can be challenging. This is particularly true for publishing journal articles, which is a common and often expected practice that involves long waiting periods, high rejection rates, and (if lucky) rounds of revisions for articles that are under consideration for being published. Prospective authors must identify journals of interest, submit manuscripts to the peer-review process, and patiently await a response. Of note, during this waiting period (i.e., while a manuscript is "under review"), authors are unable to submit the manuscript elsewhere.

Selecting Journals

Identifying journals early in the manuscript preparation process can help frame efforts to publish because authors obtain information about a journal's specifications (e.g., length) and types of content it typically publishes. Journals can be general in content (e.g., *Psychology Bulletin*) or specialized, with a focus on criminal justice (e.g., *Criminal Justice and Behavior*), law and psychology (e.g., *Law and Human Behavior*), or a more specific aspect of the field (e.g., *Psychological Injury and Law*). Journals can also publish special issues on a specific topic (e.g., homicide and the law), for which they typically put out a deadline-driven "call" to prospective authors that is circulated to certain organizations and listservs. Additional considerations include the journal's readership (i.e., the audience to which they intend to appeal), the match between your manuscript topic and the journal, how quickly the journal will make a publication decision on your manuscript (a typical standard is 2–3 months, although some journals take much longer), and the quality and reputation of the journal, including its "impact factor" (i.e., frequency of being cited elsewhere) and average rejection rates (APA, 2010). One strategy for narrowing down potential journals of interest is to note journals that often appear in a literature review on a topic related to your manuscript (Dingfelder, 2005).

Outcomes

There are three broad outcomes for a manuscript submitted to a journal: (1) rejection; (2) the opportunity to revise and resubmit the manuscript (based on reviewer feedback) before a final publication decision is made; and (3) acceptance (typically after at least one round of revisions) (APA, 2010). Most journals have submitted manuscripts reviewed by two to four peer reviewers who offer feedback on the manuscript's quality, scientific contribution, and match to the journal. The final publication decision is made by a journal editor.

REJECTION

Manuscripts may be rejected for many reasons, including serious flaws with the research design, unclear presentation of results, or awkward writing style. Manuscripts may also be rejected because they are a poor match with the journal's focus (e.g., submitting an article on psychodynamic therapy for justice-involved youth to a child neuropsychology journal) or because of a reviewer's opinion that the manuscript will not make a significantly meaningful contribution to the field.

REVISE AND RESUBMIT

In some instances, a manuscript will not be rejected or accepted, and the author is instead given an opportunity to revise the manuscript based on reviewer feedback and resubmit it for further consideration. The feedback may require major substantive changes to the manuscript, such as reorganizing the manuscript's conceptual structure or conducting additional statistical analyses, or the feedback may call for more minor revisions focused on writing style, fixing typos, and ensuring that the manuscript meets the journal's formatting requirements. In most situations, resubmitting a manuscript – even when revised based on reviewer feedback – does not guarantee the eventual acceptance of the manuscript for publication. However, being attentive and responsive to reviewer feedback will certainly increase the likelihood that the manuscript will eventually be accepted.

ACCEPTANCE

Finally, a manuscript can be accepted for publication, which of course is the goal when submitting a manuscript to a journal. Manuscripts are rarely accepted with no changes on a first submission; typically, a manuscript is accepted contingent on the author making minor revisions.

Next Steps

Persevering in the face of an undesirable response to a manuscript submission can be disheartening. If rejected, treat this as an important learning experience. Incorporate reviewer feedback and think critically about which step along the way was problematic so you can address the issue effectively moving forward (Hewlett, 2002). In this way, the manuscript preparation and submission process is similar to applying to graduate school. It is a difficult and competitive process, and rejection does not indicate that there is no good option out there.

Although the publication process can be challenging, it can be done successfully and equips students with a valuable skillset. Consider the following tips to maximize success:

- *Be mindful of timelines and timeframes*. Prepare a manuscript swiftly following completion of a research project and incorporate manuscript revisions quickly if asked to revise and resubmit.
- *Collaborate!* Various areas of expertise can provide valuable contributions to a manuscript. Involving others in the process can also stimulate progress and timely completion, and it may generate opportunities to co-author other publications.
- *Take initiative*. If you are in a program or lab that does not prioritize publishing, generate the opportunity yourself. Regularly monitor journals and keep an eye out for special issues. Revisit existing data to determine if additional hypothesis-driven analyses could potentially warrant a publication. Set writing goals for yourself and express this interest to mentors or faculty members. You are unlikely to encounter resistance if you forge ahead and create opportunities for others if your mentor or supervisor approves.
- *Try not to present on something that you do not plan to publish*. If you give a conference presentation, try to publish an article based on the presentation. Doing so maximizes on the effort you have already put into a project, which is instrumental given the limited time and resources available during graduate school.

There are several resources that offer tips on how to approach the content of a manuscript.[4] Bartol (1982) also offered insight into the "don'ts" of drafting manuscripts for publication, including an inadequate literature review, inappropriate citations, unclear information, ambiguous research questions, poorly identified samples and measures, insufficient research methodology, unclear or unreported statistical techniques or analyses, inaccurate conceptualization of the discussion, poor writing, and excessive length. Interested readers may want to check out a clever article by Martin S. Hagger titled "How to Get Your Article Rejected" (2012), which provides a tongue-in-cheek outline of things authors can do to virtually guarantee their manuscript will be rejected by a journal.

In conclusion, publications are not required to complete graduate school and obtain your doctorate degree, but they are an important step in building your career, particularly if you plan to pursue a research-based or academic career. It is a challenging process, one which should be approached strategically and from which you should not allow disappointments to dissuade you.

TEACHING, SERVICE, AND NETWORKING/COLLABORATION

The buck does not necessarily stop there if you wish to thrive in a clinical doctoral program. The things that you choose to be involved in as a graduate student can help set you up for future opportunities both during and after graduate school. One advantage of being expected to do a lot in graduate school is that it provides you with data about the things you enjoy (or do not enjoy) doing, and you also gain a clearer picture of your relative strengths and weaknesses as you enter the next phase of your career development.

Your career as a forensic psychologist can look many different ways, as can your graduate student experience. There are many doors open to you during your training, so it is important to make the most of your time. Teaching, professional development, and service to the field are valuable components of establishing yourself as a future forensic psychologist.

Teaching Opportunities

It is common for doctoral students to serve as a TA for undergraduate courses. If you think you may want to pursue a career in academics, build on this opportunity. You can also seek opportunities to be a TA at the graduate level or to independently teach undergraduate courses; these opportunities, which are less common, will equip you with an advanced and unique skillset, including creating a course syllabus, developing course content, and teaching college-level material to a variety of student populations.

Because teaching opportunities are less common and you will have other responsibilities that take priority, you should aim to teach courses that you are interested in or that fit well with your field. Additionally, if only TA opportunities are available, you may offer to teach one lecture or hold a laboratory course for the professor to gain more well-rounded experience. As a bonus, you might receive additional funding for being a TA or teaching a course.

Service Opportunities

Service opportunities are volunteer positions that support and further the field of psychology. Becoming involved in service is a great way to distinguish yourself, demonstrate a desire to contribute to the field in a meaningful way, and build your CV. One option is to serve as a student reviewer for conference proposals. When presentation proposals are submitted to the conference organizers, the proposals are typically reviewed by several people to determine if the proposal should be included as part of the conference; there are often opportunities for graduate students to review these types of proposals. You can also assist with manuscript reviews conducted by your mentor or faculty members in your program. In rare instances – and after having demonstrated competence as a manuscript reviewer – advanced graduate students may have an opportunity to independently review manuscripts submitted to a journal for publication consideration. Additionally, you can serve in student positions within professional organizations. For example, the AP-LS Student Committee works to enhance the interests of students, and the leadership positions are filled by students.

Networking/Collaboration

Throughout this chapter, we have highlighted collaboration as a way to thrive during graduate school. Networking goes hand in hand with collaboration. Both broaden the scope of the work you do, of who you know, and of what opportunities will be available to you as a graduate student and later in your career. Perhaps most notably, there will be a lot on your plate, and you may not be able to manage everything without receiving help and support from others.

Community-based

Joining local clinical organizations and attending social or professional events with graduate students from other programs is a good opportunity for networking. Doing so allows for collaboration with different departments, professionals in the field, and other students at local clinical or research placements. Additionally, joining professional organizations not only builds your skillset and knowledge base, but it introduces you to colleagues and professionals who share similar interests.

Conferences

Attending conferences is an important and common component of life as a graduate student. Conferences present yet another opportunity for networking and future collaboration. Importantly, they also allow you to gain experience presenting your own research through posters and oral presentations, and they can be a great source of inspiration for future projects. By attending major conferences in the field, such as those held by the AP-LS, International Association of Forensic Mental Health Services, and APA, you can gain visibility, meet future colleagues, learn from experts in the field, and strengthen your public-speaking skills.

Cross-disciplinary

Lastly, be creative! In a field as interdisciplinary as forensic psychology, graduate students have the unique opportunity to meet with and contribute to work done by professionals in other fields (e.g., lawyers, criminologists, sociologists, economists, probation officers). For example, there may be opportunities to attend community-based meetings about the state of the criminal justice system or other public forums to gain on-the-ground experience in this realm.

SELF-CARE AND BALANCE

As you may have gathered by now, clinical doctoral programs are challenging. Much is expected of you, and even more opportunities are available to you if you want to pursue them. Your graduate school experience can be enhanced by efforts to both survive and thrive. The graduate years are what you make of them and should be approached with the intention to build your future career as a forensic psychologist. Arguably, one of the most critical steps to survival – and often the most overlooked – is self-care.

Clinicians often advise therapy clients to regularly acknowledge their strengths, value the excess work that they put in, and practice self-care, but they often fail to take their own advice. This is directly applicable to graduate school. Burnout and feeling overwhelmed are normal. You should expect to have some moments when you question whether attending graduate school was the right choice. Instituting a regular practice of attending to and coping with the stress of graduate school is instrumental and may be the key to not only surviving, but also having the energy left to thrive.

Goal-Setting, Pacing, and Monitoring

Set goals for yourself and identify what you want from graduate school. It is never too early to begin thinking about these specifics, and it is useful to regularly reevaluate progress toward your goals and generate new goals. Doing so will help orient you to your choices in graduate school, direct your efforts, and weigh the costs and benefits of pursuing one option over another. It is important to discuss these goals with your mentors and supervisors, who can offer insight and help you achieve your goals.

Pace yourself in terms of graduate school milestones. You will be busy, often from the start of graduate school, and it is easy to fall into the trap of thinking you will have more time in the future. In fact, the idea that students and professors will have more time in the future is called the "academic fallacy." Also, much of the work you do in graduate school is self-driven and there will not always be strict deadlines for project completion. This may be a source of relief, but at the same time it requires self-discipline to accomplish what you want.

As you maintain momentum in completing graduate milestones, remember to make time for yourself and, as much as possible, prioritize interests that reduce stress and increase psychological well-being. One of the benefits of wearing many hats as a PhD student is that you can pursue responsibilities that you *enjoy* doing in addition to those that you must do. Striking this balance is important for being productive and maintaining your mental health.

Saying "No"

The bottom line is that there will always be more opportunities than you can reasonably accept in the limited time period of graduate school, particularly if having a well-rounded life is important to you. Therefore, becoming comfortable saying "no" – when appropriate, of course – is a key to success and likely one of the more important skills you can learn as a student.

When presented with an opportunity, consider what taking it means for your life months and even years from now. If you say "yes" now, what are you potentially giving up down the line? What does it mean for your current and future self? Every choice comes at the cost of something else. It is also important to consider its fit with your interests, goals, and professional development. If an opportunity does not further your interests, goals, and professional development, then it might not be worth taking. It can be particularly difficult to turn down an offer when it provides a new, rare, or unexpected opportunity, but declining to get involved in an opportunity is better than accepting the opportunity without sufficient thought and not being able to deliver.

Graduate school is a delicate balancing act in many ways – one that becomes more challenging with time as you gain greater opportunities and responsibilities. You want to balance your experiences and the time devoted to them, alongside balancing work and play. Also remember that you are not alone in this process. In addition to social support from family and friends, seek support, advice, and guidance from other students, supervisors, and mentors.

★ ★ ★

CONCLUSION

Graduate school is an extremely formative time on the road to becoming a forensic psychologist. It is challenging, requiring stamina and careful consideration. There are many details and responsibilities with which to familiarize yourself, and lots of factors to weigh when successfully completing requirements and seeking additional opportunities. Set yourself up for the career you want, work hard, and practice self-care.

Ultimately, graduate school is a finite amount of time, and it is a critical period during which you will establish the building blocks of your career. It is important to create a unique and cohesive narrative of yourself as a graduate student and future career professional. Throughout graduate school, frequently ask yourself these questions: Who do I want to be as a forensic psychologist? What impression do I want to make on my mentors and colleagues? What would I like to be doing for a career in 5 years? 10 years? 30 years?

Bear in mind that there are opportunities that are available to – and expected of – everyone in graduate school, and there are additional opportunities that are available to those who seek them out or create them. Furthermore, a clinical doctoral program is an environment in which people want to learn, grow, and innovate. Bring your ideas to your mentors and consider branching out to other departments or disciplines. Take the initiative to create a project. Remember, also, that you cannot do everything all at once. Pick and choose strategically, and learn the immense value of saying "no." Now go forth and prosper!

NOTES

1 For additional information on pre-doctoral research-based grants and fellowships available for graduate students through the National Institutes of Health or National Institute of Mental Health, see https://grants.nih.gov/grants/funding/funding_program.htm and www.nimh.nih.gov/funding/training/nimh-nrsa-practices-and-guidance.shtml
2 Integrated reports are psychological testing reports that include a review of a patient's history, clinical interview results, and a minimum of two psychological tests from one or more specific domains, including personality measures and intellectual, cognitive, and neuropsychological tests (APPIC, n.d.).
3 One example of the latter is Drexel University's Reentry Project, which was developed and implemented through the Department of Psychology and housed within the university's Psychological Services Center. The Drexel Reentry Project provides therapeutic intervention to individuals returning to the community after prison.
4 See APA (2010) for tips on what to include in and how to approach each of the traditional components of a psychology manuscript.

REFERENCES

American Psychological Association. (2006). *Guidelines and principles for accreditation of programs in professional psychology (G&P)*. Retrieved on July 20, 2019 from www.apa.org/about/policy/accreditation-archived.pdf

American Psychological Association. (2010). *Preparing manuscripts for publication in psychology journals: A guide for new authors*. Retrieved on July 20, 2019 from www.apa.org/pubs/authors/new-author-guide.pdf

American Psychological Association. (n.d.a). *Clinical psychology*. Retrieved on July 20, 2019 from www.apa.org/ed/graduate/specialize/clinical.aspx

American Psychological Association. (n.d.b). *Peer review*. Retrieved on July 20, 2019 from www.apa.org/pubs/journals/resources/peer-review.aspx

Association of Psychology Postdoctoral and Internship Centers. (n.d.). *Integrated report*. Retrieved on July 20, 2019 from www.appic.org/Internships/AAPI/Integrated-Report

Bartol, K. M. (1982). Manuscript faults and review board recommendations: Lethal and non-lethal errors. In N. F. Russo (Ed.), *Understanding the manuscript review process: Increasing the participation of women* (pp. 29–45). Washington, DC: American Psychological Association.

Burl, J., Shah, S., Filone, S., Foster, E., & DeMatteo, D. (2012). A survey of graduate training programs and coursework in forensic psychology. *Teaching of Psychology, 39*, 48–53.

DeMatteo, D., Marczyk, G., Krauss, D. A., & Burl, J. (2009). Educational and training models in forensic psychology. *Training and Education in Professional Psychology*, *3*, 184–191.

Dingfelder, S. F. (2004, April). Preparing for your comprehensive exams: Study strategically and organize citations, say faculty and students who survived the trial themselves. *GradPSYCH*. Retrieved on July 20, 2019 from www.apa.org/gradpsych/2004/04/comps.aspx

Dingfelder, S. F. (2005, January). Get published: Attaining that first manuscript acceptance takes patience and a thick skin. *GradPSYCH*. Retrieved on July 20, 2019 from www.apa.org/gradpsych/2005/01/published.aspx

Framingham, J. (2016). What is psychological assessment? *Psych Central*. Retrieved on July 20, 2019 from https://psychcentral.com/lib/what-is-psychological-assessment/

Hagger, M. S. (2012). How to get your article rejected. *Stress and Health*, *28*, 265–268.

Hatcher, R. L., Wise, E. H., & Grus, C. L. (2015). Preparation for practicum in professional psychology: A survey of training directors. *Training and Education in Professional Psychology*, *9*, 5–12.

Heilbrun, K., Rogers, R., & Otto, R. K. (2002). Forensic assessment: Current status and future directions. In J. R. P. Ogloff (Ed.), *Taking psychology and law into the twenty-first century* (pp. 119–146). Boston, MA: Springer.

Hewlett, K. (2002, September). How to publish your journal paper: Understanding the nuances of the process smooths the publishing ride. *GradPSYCH*. Retrieved on July 20, 2019 from www.apa.org/monitor/sep02/publish.aspx

Keilin, G. (2018). *2017 APPIC match: Survey of internship applicants*. Houston, TX: APPIC.

Miller v. Alabama, 567 U.S. 460, (2012).

Neal, T. M. S. (2018). Forensic psychology and correctional psychology: Distinct but related subfields of psychological science and practice. *American Psychologist*, *73*, 651–662.

Novotney, A. (2011, September). Free money for education: Check out these oft-overlooked sources of funding for psychology graduate students. *GradPSYCH Magazine*. Retrieved on July 20, 2019 from www.apa.org/gradpsych/2011/09/cover-money.aspx

Voelker, R. (2015, January). Ready for practicum? Advice on preparing for and getting the most out of your practicum experience. *GradPSYCH*. Retrieved on July 20, 2019 from www.apa.org/gradpsych/2015/01/practicum.aspx

FURTHER READING

American Psychological Association. (2010). *Preparing manuscripts for publication in psychology journals: A guide for new authors*. Retrieved on July 20, 2019 from www.apa.org/pubs/authors/new-author-guide.pdf

Ditmann, M. (2005, January). Starting the dissertation: Experts offer tips on picking a topic, conducting a lit review and narrowing your focus. *GradPSYCH*

Magazine. Retrieved on July 20, 2019 from www.apa.org/gradpsych/2005/01/starting.aspx

Novotney, A. (2016, January). Secrets for securing research funding: Apply early – and often – for success in funding your research as a graduate student, experts say. *GradPSYCH Magazine*. Retrieved on July 20, 2019 from www.apa.org/gradpsych/2016/01/research-funding.aspx

CHAPTER 7

Internship Indigestion

The preceding chapters focused on navigating the challenges associated with getting into and succeeding in graduate school. Coursework, research, conferences, publishing, and clinical practica are all vital parts of training for a forensic psychologist. After all, these experiences provide the foundation necessary for students to one day stretch their fledgling wings and take off on their own, out from under the purview of their mentors and academic support networks. Fortunately, there is a transition period – internship – between being a student and a professional that allows students to further develop into competent, independent psychologists.

At its core, internship is a formalized program of paid clinical work experience designed to allow students to switch their focus from juggling research, courses, and practicum to focusing almost exclusively on the practice of clinical psychology. Students in applied doctoral programs are required to complete an internship, whereas students in purely research-based doctoral programs are not required to complete an internship because they do not provide clinical services and do not get licensed as psychologists (see Chapter 9 for more discussion regarding licensure). During internship, students work full-time in clinical settings under the supervision of doctoral-level psychologists learning how to function as an autonomous professional. The goal is to enable students to sharpen, fine-tune, and master the clinical and critical-thinking skills obtained during the coursework and practicum years of graduate school.

The internship process can be likened to learning to ride a bicycle. The courses and practica completed during graduate school can be thought of as the training wheels stage. Training wheels allow aspiring cyclists to get used to the feel of sitting on a bike, turning the pedals, and steering, with the stability of four wheels on the ground to ensure the bike does not topple over before the rider is able to master the process. Similarly, practicum allows students to practice translating the therapeutic and assessment skills they learn in class to real-word clinical settings, but with the stability of close supervision and training by a licensed professional.

Internship can be conceptualized as the progression from training wheels to riding a bike independently. When learning to ride a bike, aspiring cyclists initially require training wheels and a guiding hand. These supports are withdrawn over time as the cyclist demonstrates mastery of the machine and the ability to ride independently. Similarly, students on internship are placed in clinical situations in which they bear a large amount of responsibility under close supervision. As interns demonstrate aptitude for clinical practice, supervisors gradually scale back the level of support provided, leaving the intern to function more independently.

The internship process can be exciting, but few things are as daunting as the dreaded internship application process. As such, the focus of this chapter is on helping aspiring forensic psychologists to navigate this critical step toward obtaining a doctoral degree. In this chapter, we address things to consider in preparation for internship, an overview of the internship application process and match process, tips for approaching interviews, and things to consider between matching and starting internship.

LAYING THE GROUNDWORK: CONSIDERATIONS DURING PRACTICUM YEARS

> If you fail to plan, you are planning to fail.
> – Benjamin Franklin

Maybe Benjamin Franklin's sage cautionary advice is not quite as dire in the internship context as it is in other life contexts, but it certainly has some applicability. If students gain clinical experience via practicum and complete the requirements of their graduate program, they are well positioned to obtain an internship. However, students should be mindful early in graduate school regarding what they might want their internship experience to look like, and mindful of doing prep work to make the application process run as smoothly as possible. Below are two key considerations for the early years of graduate school.

What type of practicum experiences are you pursuing? As previously noted, practicum provides students with clinical experience during graduate school. However, the types of clinical experiences students obtain in graduate school will have some bearing on the types of internship sites for which they will be competitive and to which internship sites they would like to apply. Internship sites encompass many clinical settings, demand varied types of clinical skillsets, and cater to diverse clinical populations. Many internship sites seek applicants with a demonstrated interest in and experience with the population, settings, and clinical work to which the site caters. As such, students who have an idea of the type of internship site they would like to work in may benefit from pursuing practicum placements that provide a solid foundation for entry into that site, either through direct experience or the development of transferable skills. For example, students targeting forensic internship sites may want to complete a practicum that offers some exposure to forensic populations, such as practica at a state hospital, forensic assessment clinic, or correctional facility. These and other examples were explored in more depth in Chapter 6.

Tracking hours. Given the expectation that students have clinical experience prior to beginning internship, it should come as little surprise that part of the internship application process is numerically accounting for prior clinical experience. Internship sites are interested in quantification of clinical experience across a number of domains, including total clinical hours, hours devoted to therapy/intervention, hours devoted to assessment, number of individuals to whom services have been provided, number of therapy groups facilitated/led, demographic information of clients, testing measures administered, integrated reports written, supervision hours, and support hours. Attempting to reconstruct this information from memory shortly before submitting internship applications can prove difficult, so students are advised to track their clinical experiences in real time. A handful of companies/organizations have developed software programs to help students to track their hours, although students may also construct their own tracking systems.

An **integrated report** is "a report that includes a review of history, results of an interview and at least two psychological tests from one or more of the following categories: personality measures, intellectual tests, cognitive tests, and neuropsychological tests" (APPIC, n.d.).

DOOMSDAY PREPARATIONS: PRE-APPLICATION CONSIDERATIONS

For the doctoral psychology student, internship serves two purposes. First, it is one of the final boxes to check off before students finally earn their doctoral degree. Second, it furthers students' training goals, whether they include receiving more in-depth training in an area already familiar to them, gaining a skillset they are lacking, or applying skills practiced with one patient population to a different patient population. In this way, internship is a personal experience tailored to the unique needs of each student. Besides being one of the final steps (often along with defending a dissertation) before earning a doctoral degree, the internship process requires students to reflect on training goals – and life goals – before submitting internship applications. This section focuses on factors to consider before determining to which internship sites to apply.

What are your training goals? Perhaps the greatest pre-application consideration relates to training goals. Internship sites vary widely in terms of experiences offered (e.g., therapy, assessment, research, didactics), populations served (e.g., children, college students, adults, individuals with severe mental illness, criminal offenders), settings (e.g., outpatient, inpatient, forensic, correctional), workload, and time commitment. Further, prospective interns come from a wide variety of backgrounds and interests. Some students view internship as a way to gain additional experience in an area in which they have already specialized, while others view it as an opportunity to fill a perceived training gap or to begin working towards specialization in a certain area or with a certain population. Others take the approach of completing internship in a setting or subfield in which they *think* they want to pursue a career to confirm whether their inklings are correct. Still others have no real preference as long as they secure an internship, get their doctorate, and move on to the next phase of their career. Whatever the motivation for internship, some healthy self-reflection about your training goals and what you hope to gain from internship is key in deciding to which types of sites to apply.

What is your current life situation? Another consideration in applying to internship is your current life situation. Students come from a variety of family and financial backgrounds that can impact their application strategy. For example, students who are not tethered to any relationship or family attachments may not be geographically restricted in applying to sites. These individuals may be more mobile and able to apply to sites throughout the United States and Canada. Students in relationships and/or with families or other attachments may be less willing to relocate to far-away locations.

Similar concerns present themselves depending on students' financial situations. The internship application process varies widely in terms of cost, depending on the application strategy. Applicants must register for the internship match via the National Matching Services, with associated fees typically exceeding $100. Additionally, students apply to internship sites through the Association of Psychology Postdoctoral and Internship Centers' (APPIC) centralized APPIC Application for Psychology Internships (AAPI). There is a fee associated with each application submitted through AAPI. Given that students typically apply to 10–15 internship sites (Keilin, 2018), submitting applications can cost several hundred dollars, and interviews can significantly compound costs. In recent years, students have received an average of seven interview offers per application cycle (Keilin, 2018). Interviewing at sites far away from one's school may require numerous flights, hotel rooms, and rental cars.

An additional financial consideration is the anticipated internship salary. As noted earlier, internship functions as a form of paid work experience, with emphasis placed on the experience obtained, not on the amount of money earned. Average salaries during internship – though often higher than graduate stipends and surely higher than the negative income incurred by taking on more debt – are still fairly low, hovering between $25,000 and $30,000 (Keilin, 2018). That said, sites vary widely in terms of salaries and the cost of living associated with the area in which they are located. Students seeking greater financial freedom may choose to target sites with higher salaries, or sites in locations where money can be stretched further. For example, Federal Bureau of Prisons (BOP) sites offer compensation on the higher end of the scale.

PRE-INTERNSHIP CONSIDERATIONS

- Training goals (desired experiences, clinical populations, and training settings)
- Current life situation (geographic or financial restrictions)
- Postdoctoral fellowship and career aspirations

What are my goals for after internship? Technically, internship represents the culmination of students' graduate training. Next stop – the real world! Therefore, it is important for applicants to give thought to what they might want their lives to look like after completing internship. A common consideration for students is where they might want to live post-internship. For students targeting a specific geographic area for their career, it may be wise to apply to internship sites near that area. This may make it easier to facilitate travel for job interviews and allow for the development of a professional network in that area. Additionally, students at some internship sites accept postdoctoral positions or jobs at the same site, which adds further credence to a strategy of applying to a site located in an area where the student wants to be long-term. For example, some state hospitals offer jobs as a psychology associate (an unlicensed clinician operating under the supervision of a licensed psychologist) to former interns, which can lead to full-time positions upon licensure.

THE PARADOX OF CHOICE: NARROWING YOUR INTERNSHIP SITE LIST

The internship application process – like all application processes – begins by figuring out to which sites to apply. For those familiar with Dr. Barry Schwartz's (2016) paradox of choice phenomena – in which greater breadth of selection can yield decisional paralysis – this can be an arduous task. To maximize chances of matching, students are encouraged to apply to 10–15 internship sites (Chamberlin, 2009), but narrowing down the list of potential sites can be challenging because there are hundreds of internships sites. Several considerations are presented below, with a focus on maximizing one's chances of matching.

Is the site a good fit? Perhaps the most important consideration in identifying potential internship sites is whether the site is a good "fit" for the student's interests and experience. Ideally, students should apply to sites that "complement their training goals, personality styles, and other fit-factors" (Chamberlin, 2009, p. 36). Applicants who apply to sites for which they are not a great fit often do not receive interview offers from those sites. "Fit" is somewhat of an amorphous construct and can be demonstrated in numerous ways. One way is to select sites that mirror one's previous clinical experiences. For example, students with experience working with individuals with severe mental illness may be a better fit for a state hospital site. Similarly, a student who completed a practicum placement or held a job in a correctional setting might be a better fit for a correctional internship site than a student with no prior correctional experience.

Applying to internships that mirror one's clinical experience is not the only strategy to facilitate fit. Another application strategy is to select sites that offer an experience that fills a training gap. This may be particularly helpful when applying to more specialized internship sites. Time in graduate school is limited, and students often forgo some experiences in which they would be interested. Fortunately, internship sites recognize that specialized training may not be widely offered during the practicum training years. To this end, students might apply to an internship that is outside the realm of their previous clinical experience, making it clear that they are seeking exposure to an area of interest with which they had not previously been able to gain experience. In addition to communicating their interest, students may want to emphasize any transferable skills from previous clinical experiences that would facilitate quick growth in a new context. For example, a student with outpatient experience with clients with severe mental illness who is interested in a state hospital setting might emphasize that he or she previously worked with individuals with severe mental illness and is interested in exploring how inpatient treatment differs from outpatient treatment for this population.

STRATEGIES TO FACILITATE "FIT"

- Apply to sites where the work mirrors your prior clinical experiences
- Apply to sites where the work fills a training gap
- Apply to sites that match well with your life circumstances (e.g., geographic preferences)

In considering fit, students must consider their life circumstances. As noted, some students with ties to a geographic area may be hesitant to relocate. Depending on the geographic area, a geographic restriction may greatly reduce the number of available training sites that complement the applicant's clinical interests and experiences. A mistake some applicants make is applying to 10–15 sites in one geographic area under the assumption that applying to the recommended number of sites will ensure a match. Applying to sites that simply reflect your geographic preference – as opposed to sites that may be more spread out but a better fit with your clinical strengths and skills – appreciably reduces the chances of matching (Chamberlin, 2009).

Students do not necessarily have to be willing to move across the country, but they should be open to the idea of moving more generally.

Due to the availability of opportunities, students living in rural areas may need to extend their geographic radius more than students living in more urban areas. For example, a student interested in a forensically oriented internship who lives in a rural area with limited opportunities may need to be willing to move to an area that offers more opportunities. In contrast, applicants in New York City or Boston who are interested in a forensically oriented internship may be able to restrict their search to sites within a few hours away given the density of forensically oriented internship sites on the East Coast.

Are you looking specifically for forensic experience on internship? Students interested in becoming a forensic psychologist are not required to get forensic training during internship. There are many paths to obtaining specialized forensic training and receiving training on internship is only one such path. Internship sites vary widely in the forensic experiences they offer. Some offer a formalized forensic track or rotation, while others do not offer direct forensic experience but instead forensically relevant experience, such as conducting assessments with clients who are justice-involved. They also vary widely in terms of the settings in which forensic work is conducted. Common settings for forensic internship sites include state hospitals, correctional facilities, consortiums, medical schools, and community mental health centers.

There are several resources available to help applicants identify programs that offer forensic training. The APPIC website (www.appic.org/) hosts a directory of its internship sites, searchable through keywords associated with the site, specific terms within a program's description, or selecting a specific training opportunity, such as "forensics/corrections." Additionally, the American Psychology-Law Society Student Committee (www.apls-students.org/) maintains an annually updated database of sites that offer significant forensic experience and training.

Is the site accredited by the American Psychological Association (APA) or Canadian Psychological Association (CPA)? Similar to the considerations for choosing an appropriate graduate program (see Chapter 4), accreditation is an element to consider when applying for internship. Many graduate programs require that students complete an *accredited* internship as a graduation requirement, meaning that attending a *non-accredited* internship may result in students not obtaining their degree. Similarly, state licensing boards require students to complete internship programs that meet a certain minimum standard of quality – something that is much easier to ensure when coming from an accredited program (Bailey, 2004).

Where would I like to become licensed? Jurisdictions require varying numbers of supervised work hours to be eligible for licensure, typically hovering between 2,000 and 4,000 hours. Many jurisdictions allow for hours accumulated during internship to count towards that total. Internships offer varying numbers of supervised hours, but to meet APPIC requirements for membership – keeping in mind that not all internship sites are APPIC members – the site must offer a minimum of 1,500 supervised work hours. This minimum number of hours would be insufficient for licensure eligibility in most jurisdictions, so students would need to gain additional supervised work experience before being eligible for licensure in those jurisdictions. Therefore, students who plan to become licensed in jurisdictions that require a greater number of supervised work hours may want to target internship sites that offer enough supervised hours.

What does my graduate program require in terms of internship training? Graduate programs specify the types of internships that will satisfy the requirements for obtaining a doctoral degree. Two common requirements include attending an APA/CPA-accredited internship program and obtaining a certain number of supervised work hours on internship. For students whose programs require attending an accredited internship program, they can narrow their list by removing from consideration any non-accredited programs. The requirement for obtaining a certain number of hours is less black and white because some sites may be willing to provide additional experience for students based on their graduation requirements.

Do my lifestyle and history mesh with the requirements of the internship site? This consideration is multi-faceted. As emphasized throughout this chapter, internship experiences vary widely. Some sites are workhorse-style sites, requiring interns to put in long hours, while others may follow a more traditional 40-hour work week. Applicants who value a strong work–life balance may want to consider the workload expectations of sites. An applicant's lifestyle and background are also relevant to this discussion. Some internships require applicants to pass a drug test or a background screen before they can begin working, and many sites require interns to pass a criminal background check. Often, drug tests or criminal background checks do not occur until after students have already matched to a site, and failing either one can result in termination of an offer (APPIC, 2018b).

THE APPLICATION PROCESS

The internship application process is often a source of stress for doctoral students. Fear not! This section gives you an overview of the application process to facilitate preparation and minimize surprises.

The application process is split into Phases I and II. Phase I applies to all applicants, while Phase II pertains to applicants who did not match in Phase I. In Phase I, all applicants prepare a centralized application called the AAPI. There are several aspects to the AAPI. First, there is a general application in which applicants provide demographic information and information regarding their education and clinical/practicum experience. Reporting clinical experience includes an accounting of the number of clients seen and/or groups led, clinical settings (inpatient vs. outpatient), client demographics, and type of interaction (intervention vs. assessment). Applicants also document their psychological testing experience and the number of assessment and integrated reports they have written. The generalized application also includes several essay questions. The current essay questions focus on the applicant's autobiographical history, theoretical orientation, view of diversity in clinical practice, and research interests.

Second, the AAPI requires supplemental materials that are either directly uploaded by the applicant or independently submitted to APPIC by a third party. These materials include:

- a cover letter, ideally tailored to each site (uploaded by applicant);
- a curriculum vitae (CV) describing one's education, clinical training/experience, research training/experience, presentations and publications, teaching experience, work experience, and special recognitions (uploaded by applicant);
- official academic transcripts from all graduate institutions attended (requested from each institution);
- recommendation letters (uploaded by each recommender to ensure confidentiality); and
- a clinical writing sample, typically a case summary of a therapy case or a psychological evaluation (varies by site).

Most of the AAPI is relatively straightforward, albeit tedious, but the essays and supplemental materials require more planning. Internship directors value essays because they provide a glimpse into an applicant's personality. Applicants sometimes struggle with essays, finding it difficult to write about their lives, interests, and approaches to clinical work. As noted in prior chapters, it is important to remain professional when writing essays. Self-disclosure – even if it appears to be pulled for by an essay (such as the autobiographical essay) – must be properly restrained. Discussing a work experience that spurred your interest in psychology is one thing; describing serious life challenges that you would only disclose to your family or a trusted friend is ill advised. It is often helpful to have supervisors, academic mentors, and/or trusted peers review your essays and provide feedback, which requires advanced planning.

Cover letters can be time consuming to write, particularly when trying to tailor each letter to a specific site. However, for students who apply to similar types of sites, the cover letters may follow the same template and only vary to the extent that they discuss site-specific training goals or relevant clinical experiences. Because tailoring cover letters can be time consuming, early planning is important.

Transcripts are often mailed to APPIC (although some institutions have electronic agreements with APPIC), which uploads them to the AAPI for applicants. As such, it is important to request transcripts well in advance of application deadlines to allow for adequate time to upload and troubleshoot any issues that arise. Similar concerns apply to letters of recommendation. It is important to identify individuals who can speak to your qualifications that are relevant to internship – namely, clinical experience and graduate school performance. It is equally important to provide recommenders with adequate time to write their letters, particularly because other students are also likely asking them for letters.

For sites that require writing samples, such as a client testing report, all materials must be redacted in accordance with the Health Insurance Portability and Accountability Act of 1996 (HIPAA) (APPIC, 2012). Submitting samples that contain clients' identifying information can result in the disqualification of an applicant. As such, applicants need to set aside enough time to thoroughly review all samples to ensure they are HIPAA-compliant.

Interviews

After applications have been submitted and reviewed, interview offers are extended by sites. Several internship interview considerations overlap with the interview guidance provided in previous chapters, but there is some internship-specific guidance we can provide. As a starting point, it is important to do some background prep work and be familiar with each site before the interview. Doing so allows you to demonstrate your knowledge of the site and ask questions that are relevant to that site. Sites often consider whether applicants have long-term clinical interests that match those of the site. Also, practice is key. Being thoroughly prepared for the common questions that are asked during internship interviews helps to increase confidence, ensure substantive instead of superficial answers, and facilitate smooth delivery.

COMMON INTERVIEW QUESTION TOPICS

- Challenging clinical experiences with clients
- Ethical dilemmas encountered and their resolution
- Long-term career interests
- Specific interests in that site
- Research interests

It is important to be yourself on interviews. A common internship cliché is that students are interviewing the sites just as much as the sites are interviewing them. As with many clichés, this one (largely) is true! Ideally, you want to intern at a site where you will enjoy the work and enjoy working with the supervisors and other clinical staff. As such, students should get a sense of whether the site is some place they would like to work. With that said, applicants who come across as entitled will likely be negatively viewed by internship sites; it is important to remain professional, polite, and respectful while gathering information about the internship site.

Speaking with current interns is a good idea. Current interns can provide the best sense of what being an intern at that site is truly like. Many sites encourage current interns to be as honest as possible with applicants and will schedule time for applicants to meet with interns in more informal (though still professional) interactions.

Gaining a sense of the clinical responsibilities at an internship is important to help you determine if the training provided by the site is consistent with your experience and skill level. Some students may be more advanced in their forensic training and experience, particularly if they completed forensic practica or come from a forensic psychology graduate program. For applicants with lots of experience conducting clinical interviews, administering forensic and other psychological tests, and writing forensic reports, it may not be desirable to attend a program where interns are expected largely to shadow forensic psychologists as opposed to having some independent responsibility. However, applicants with relatively little forensic experience may want to avoid a site that expects its interns to function more independently.

Finally, it is important to take some notes and follow up with internship sites. Creating real-time notes about aspects of the internship site that you like or did not like will help you to formulate your rankings lists. Interviews take place from mid-December to late January – and applicants may have multiple interviews – so the interview experiences can start to blend together, which highlights the importance of taking notes about each site. Additionally, a follow-up e-mail is typically a good idea. A brief e-mail allows you to get any remaining questions answered, further communicate your interest in a site, and exhibit an extra degree of professionalism.

Ranking and Matching

After interviews are completed, the ranking and match process begins. Students and internship sites both generate rank-order lists that they submit to APPIC; pairings can only occur if a site and a student have both included one another on the ranking list. APPIC uses an algorithm to optimize pairings based on the preferences of both parties. Results are provided to students (typically via e-mail) according to a uniform notification date. If a student does not match, he or she can enter Phase II of the match and apply for any unfilled internship spots. Phase II of the match functions much the same way as Phase I, with minor changes that will not be expanded upon here (see the Further Reading list for additional information) (APPIC, 2018a).

Ranking sites requires some extra discussion. The best advice is to simply rank sites that best fit your interests and goals. Aspiring forensic psychologists can apply to a variety of sites that provide forensic or forensically relevant experience, including state or federal correctional sites, state hospitals, university-based clinics, and academic medical centers. For applicants interested in a career with the Federal BOP, it might be advisable to rank any BOP sites toward the top of the list because interning at a BOP site can serve as a gateway to a permanent position. Similarly, if an applicant eventually wants to work in a state hospital, it might be better to rank those types of sites higher than others. Postdoctoral aspirations may also be a factor. Some internship sites also offer postdoctoral positions, so highly ranking one of those internship sites may be beneficial if you might want to stay there for a postdoc.

POST-MATCH CONSIDERATIONS

Congratulations! You have completed the arduous and stressful process of applying to internship. The hay is in the barn, right? Not quite yet! There are still several considerations to address before beginning internship.

First, dissertation, dissertation, dissertation. Completing a dissertation during internship can be challenging (Krieshok, Lopez, Somberg, & Cantrell, 2000). As such, many graduate programs require that students begin their dissertations as a prerequisite for applying to internship. Having your dissertation completed – or at least well under way – frees up a lot of time, which reduces stress and opens up opportunities to take advantage of other experiences internship may provide. Also, some internships allow interns to spend a certain amount of time each week (typically 4–8 hours) working on research, including their dissertation.

Second, it is important to start making plans for relocating if students match to an internship that requires them to move. Internships can start any time from mid-June to early September, and some students may have graduate school commitments that continue right up to the beginning of internship. Negotiating earlier terminations of these commitments if necessary is important, particularly when trying to uphold professionalism. Setting aside time to look for housing – often after reaching out to current interns or staff at your future internship site – is key. Match day is typically at the end of February, so students may only have a few months to figure out living arrangements. Additionally, it is important to consider self-care. Burnout in graduate school is real, and internship may be a continuation of burning the candle at both ends. For internship sites with later start dates, the internship may end and a postdoctoral fellowship or job might begin almost immediately. Taking some time to recharge before (and/or after) internship is advisable.

KEY CONSIDERATIONS AFTER THE MATCH

- Completing – or having made substantial progress on – your dissertation
- Terminating existing commitments in a professional manner
- Relocation plans

★ ★ ★

CONCLUSION

This chapter provided an overview of internship, including pre-application considerations, choosing internship sites to which to apply, the internship application process, and post-match considerations. There are several main takeaways from this chapter:

- Internship can serve numerous purposes. At a minimum, it is a required part of graduate programs in applied psychology (i.e., those specialty areas of psychology in which psychologists provide clinical services). It can also enable students to gain specialized experience with forensic populations and determine if forensic psychology is truly where their practice interests lie. Alternatively, internship can be used to fill in gaps in training or to gain more generalist training before moving towards specialization.

- In selecting internship sites to which to apply, it is important to consider your overall career goals. Do you want to work in a particular clinical setting? Are you targeting a certain geographic area for your career? If so, it might be advisable to explore what sites in that geographic area offer forensic training, and, if there are limited options, how you might obtain the specialized experience that forensic psychology requires. The key in selecting sites is fit. Fit can include applying to sites that reflect your prior experiences or to sites that will fill a training gap. Current life situation might also factor into fit. If finances are a concern, it may be advisable to apply to sites on the higher end of the pay scale or in geographic areas with a lower cost of living.

- The internship application process is managed by APPIC. Components of the internship application include the general APPIC application, essays, official graduate transcripts, recommendation letters, and possibly clinical writing samples. After applications are submitted, applicants may be asked to interview at some sites, and then both students and sites submit ranking lists. APPIC uses an algorithm to ensure optimal match outcomes for students and sites.

- After the match, it is important for students to plan for the transition into internship, including potential relocation and completing/continuing their dissertation.

REFERENCES

Association of Psychology Postdoctoral and Internship Centers. (2012, July 1). *APPIC policy on AAPI online supplemental materials*. Retrieved on July 20, 2019 from www.appic.org/Internships/AAPI/AAPI-Supplemental-Materials-Policy.

Association of Psychology Postdoctoral and Internship Centers. (2018a, December 29). *Frequently asked questions: Internship applicants – Match eligibility & participation*. Retrieved on July 20, 2019 from www.appic.org/Match/FAQs/Applicants/Eligibility-and-Participation.

Association of Psychology Postdoctoral and Internship Centers. (2018b, December 29). *Frequently asked questions: Internship training directors – preparing for the Match*. Retrieved on July 20, 2019 from www.appic.org/Match/FAQs/Training-Directors/Preparing-for-the-Match.

Association of Psychology Postdoctoral and Internship Centers. (n.d.). *Integrated report*. Retrieved on July 20, 2019 from www.appic.org/Internships/AAPI/Integrated-Report.

Bailey, D. S. (2004, April). Why accreditation matters. *gradPSYCH Magazine, 2* (2).Retrieved on July 20, 2019 from www.apa.org/gradpsych/2004/04/accreditation

Chamberlin, J. (2009, September). Match day mythology. *gradPYSCH Magazine*, 7(3), 36.

Keilin, G. (2018). *2018 APPIC Match: survey of internship applicants part 1-summary of survey results*. Retrieved on July 20, 2019 from https://appic.org/Internships/Match/Match-Statistics/Applicant-Survey-2018-Part-1

Krieshok, T. S., Lopez, S. J., Somberg, D. R., & Cantrell, P. J. (2000). Dissertation while on internship: Obstacles and predictors of progress. *Professional Psychology: Research and Practice, 31*, 327–331.

Schwartz, B. (2016). *The paradox of choice: why more is less* (Rev. ed). New York: HarperCollins Publishers, Inc.

FURTHER READING

American Psychological Association. (n.d.). *Ending the internship crisis*. Retrieved on July 20, 2019 from www.apa.org/apags/resources/internship-crisis.

Association of Psychology Postdoctoral and Internship Centers. (2018, December 26). *The APPIC Match: Phase II: "Getting started" guide for applicants*. Retrieved on July 20, 2019 from www.appic.org/Internships/Match/APPIC-Match-Phase-II/Phase-II-Getting-started.

Carver, K. S. (2015, May). *What is the most common mistake you see in internship applications?: How to avoid pitfalls of internship applications. Div. 18 Student Newsletter*. Retrieved on July 20, 2019 from www.apadivisions.org/division-18/publications/newsletters/student/2015/05/internship-applications.

Clark, J. C. (2011). Answer these 5: Know these questions to ace your internship interviews. *gradPSYCH Magazine, 9*(1), 20.

Dingfelder, S. F. (2005, September). Pulling away from the pack: Training directors offer tips on writing winning internship application essays. *gradPSYCH Magazine, 3*(3). Retrieved on July 20, 2019 from www.apa.org/gradpsych/2005/09/pulling.

Greer, M. (2004). Put your best foot forward in internship interviews: Experts share secrets on making a strong impression in internship interviews. *gradPSYCH Magazine, 2*(4).Retrieved on July 20, 2019 from www.apa.org/gradpsych/2004/09/bestfoot.

Leis-Newman, E. (2011). Just do it: there are significant benefits to finishing your dissertation before starting your internship including better finances, more research opportunities, better focus and being near your support system. *gradPSYCH Magazine, 9*(2), 18.

Madson, M. B., Hasan, N. T., Williams-Nickelson, C., Kettmann, J., & Van Sickle, K. S. (2007). The internship supply and demand issue: Graduate student's perspective. *Training and Education in Professional Psychology, 1*, 249–257.

McCutcheon, S. (2011). The internship crisis: An uncommon urgency to build a common solution. *Training and Education in Professional Psychology*, *5*, 144–148.

Mellott, R. N., Arden, I. A., & Cho, M. E. (1997). Preparing for internship: Tips for the prospective applicant. *Professional Psychology: Research and Practice*, *28*, 190–196.

National Matching Services, Inc. (n.d.) *Matching algorithm: The 2019 APPIC Match*. Retrieved on July 20, 2019 from https://natmatch.com/psychint/algorithm.html.

Norcross, J. C., Ellis, J. L., & Sayette, M. A. (2010). Getting in and getting money: A comparative analysis of admission standards, acceptance rates, and financial assistance across the research-practice continuum in clinical psychology programs. *Training and Education in Professional Psychology*, *4*, 99–104.

Parent, M. C., Bradstreet, T. C., Wood, M., Ameen, E., & Callahan, J. C. (2016). "The worst experience of my life": The Internship crisis and its impact on students. *Journal of Clinical Psychology*, *72*, 714–742.

Tartakovsky, M. (2018, October 8). *8 hints for selecting an internship site*. Retrieved on July 20, 2019 from https://psychcentral.com/lib/8-hints-for-selecting-an-internship-site/.

Tartakovsky, M. (2018, October 8). *9 ideas for increasing your chances of matching*. Retrieved from https://psychcentral.com/lib/9-ideas-for-increasing-your-chances-of-matching/.

Wells, S. C., Herbst, R. B., Parent, M. C., Ameen, E. J., El-Ghoroury, N. H., Mattu, A. M., … Fitzgerald, M. E. (2014). The Internship crisis: Graduate students look back and plan ahead. *Training and Education in Professional Psychology*, *8*, 112–118.

Part III

Professional Puzzles

CHAPTER 8

Postdoc Pandemonium

As discussed in earlier chapters, there are multiple paths individuals can follow to acquire forensic specialization. A postdoctoral fellowship – often referred to as "postdoc" – is the final dedicated formalized training in pursuit of that goal. Like internship, postdoc consists of paid work experience, but unlike internship, the purpose of postdoc is not to become adept at generalized clinical practice but rather to move towards a specialty area or to facilitate re-specialization. Psychologists enter a postdoc having already completed their degrees and under the assumption that they possess a base level of general clinical skills, and they complete a postdoc to move towards mastery in a specific specialty area of psychology.

This chapter explores the postdoc process, providing readers with guidance regarding how to identify postdoc sites, approach the application process, and select the site that best fits their goals. The internship and postdoc processes overlap substantially. For the sake of brevity, only aspects of the postdoc process that are distinct from the internship process will be explored in detail. The purpose of postdoc is specialization (and sometimes re-specialization), so only considerations relevant to forensic postdocs – as opposed to postdocs in other specialty areas of psychology – are discussed. Additionally, we will describe alternative post-graduate options for obtaining specialized clinical training.

FELLOWSHIP FAST FACTS

In broad terms, there are two types of postdocs: clinical postdocs and research postdocs. Clinical postdocs help trainees to hone the skills that are necessary for specialized clinical practice in a recognized specialty area, such as forensic psychology or clinical neuropsychology. Many clinical postdocs are housed in sites similar to those of internship programs (e.g., state hospitals, outpatient clinics). In contrast, research postdocs focus on helping individuals to hone skills in a specific research area (e.g., addiction treatment) and to become more adept at securing grant funding for their research. These postdocs tend to be housed in universities or academic medical centers (Forand & Applebaum, 2011). Regardless of the type, postdocs are typically 1 or 2 years in duration (DeMatteo, Marczyk, Krauss, & Burl, 2009).

SINGULARITIES AND SIMILARITIES: A COMPARISON TO INTERNSHIP

Internship vs. Postdoc: A Comparison

Internship	Postdoc
• Required part of training	• Not required part of training
• Requires supervision	• Requires supervision
• Application through APPIC	• More informal application process
• Match system	• Timeline system

Singularity – Is postdoc required? Simply put, the answer is "no." This is a key distinction between internships and postdocs. Internship is required for clinical psychology doctoral students to earn their degrees and seek licensure, and some specialty areas of psychology, such as neuropsychology, require the completion of a postdoc, but a postdoc is not required to become a forensic psychologist. Although most jurisdictions require licensure candidates to obtain a set number of supervised clinical hours beyond those gained during internship to be eligible for licensure, few jurisdictions require licensure applicants to complete a formal postdoc. Supervised clinical hours can be obtained in the workforce rather than via a formal postdoc, and benefits to the workforce approach include a higher salary and greater variety in professional opportunities. Because of this, psychologists may choose to enter the workforce after graduation. However, notable drawbacks to completing an informal postdoc include a lack of training depth/focus and the possible lack of a mentor–mentee relationship that can help emerging psychologists to cement their professional identities (Bailey, 2004a).

Similarity – Do I still need supervision? "Yes" – at least if you are completing a formal postdoc. The premise of internship is to allow graduate students to gain supervised clinical experience in furtherance of general practice competence. Formal postdocs provide a similar opportunity, but by choice rather than necessity. Although postdoctoral fellows in some jurisdictions may become licensed during their postdoc, this does not relieve them of the need for supervision if they agreed to be supervised as part of a formal postdoc. Licensed psychologists are legally capable of assuming full responsibility for their clients, but individuals completing a formal postdoc continue to receive supervision as part of their training experience.

Similarity – Are the search strategies the same? Largely, "yes"! As with internship, there are two primary databases for identifying forensic psychology postdoctoral positions – the Association of Psychology Postdoctoral and Internship Centers' (APPIC) Universal Psychology Postdoctoral Directory and the American Psychology-Law Society (AP-LS) website. Other postdoc databases might be found via the Association for Psychological Science postdoc exchange, the career section of the website for *Science* magazine, The Psychology Job Wiki, or the website for the American Psychological Association (APA) ("How to find a postdoc," 2014).

However, some forensic postdocs are not listed in any database, so consulting outside resources, such as school/professional listservs, state job directories, or job search websites (e.g., Monster, Glassdoor), may supplement your postdoc search. Further, some postdocs may recruit candidates via associated internship sites by asking internship training directors to disseminate information about the postdoc. Lastly, tapping into one's existing professional network – particularly at psychology conferences – may prove fruitful (Kuo, 2012;).

Similarity – You mean I still need cover letters, personal statements, letters of recommendation, writing samples, a curriculum vitae (CV) ...? Affirmative. Like the internship process, the postdoc application process is best conceptualized as applying for a job. To be competitive, postdoc applicants need to demonstrate interest in and fit with a site. This is accomplished through cover letters tailored to each specific site that highlight your interests and qualifications; a CV that chronicles your professional experiences, including internship experiences; letters of recommendation, ideally from at least one supervisor or mentor familiar with your forensic experiences or transferable skills; and writing samples, such as a forensic assessment report.

Singularity – Do I need to complete the APPIC application process? Most likely not. Unlike internship, many forensic postdocs do not require the submission of applications through the APPIC portal. Application materials are typically requested via e-mail, which reduces costs as applicants do not incur any type of application submission or processing fees. Additional benefits include a more direct line of communication with postdoc sites and a less formal approach to interview offers and scheduling.

Similarity – Are the application and interview timelines roughly the same? Roughly "yes," with heavy emphasis on "roughly." For internship, applications tend to be due by mid-November, with interviews in December and January. For postdoc, this timeline is usually pushed back approximately 1 month, but some deadlines may be as late as March (Forand & Applebaum, 2011). Typically, postdoc interviews occur in January and February, with offers extended at the end of February (Novotney, 2017). Of note, postdoc offerings may occur on a rolling basis, which results in greater variability in the application and interview dates.

Singularity – Is there a postdoc match system? Not exactly! Unlike internship, many forensic postdocs do not require applications via APPIC. Those that require formal applications via APPIC tend to adhere to the Uniform Notification Deadline (UND), in which sites agree not to extend offers to applicants prior to a specified date and time. Recognizing that many sites do not follow the UND, the UND guidelines allow individuals receiving offers prior to the UND to request reciprocal offers from their top-ranked site. If the top-ranked site extends an offer, applicants must accept the offer immediately.

Other forensic postdoctoral programs adhere to the Uniform Acceptance Date (UAD), in which programs agree to extend offers prior to a specified date and time. Although offers can be extended prior to this date and time, sites cannot require applicants to accept an offer before the UAD. Like the UND, applicants who receive offers from one program but have yet to hear from their top choice can contact that program to request a reciprocal offer, which is mandatory to accept if provided. Under the UAD, applicants can only hold one offer at a time and must withdraw from consideration at all sites on their list ranked lower than a site from which they are holding an offer. Of note, this list is not a formal ranking list that needs to be submitted in the way that a ranking list must be submitted as part of the internship application process. Some postdoc programs set their own internal deadlines and timelines for decisions once offers are made. When considering postdoc sites, it is important to be aware of each site's timeline because it can be tricky to manage offers from sites with variable timeframes and conditions for extending and accepting offers.

APPLICATION TIMELINES

Uniform Notification Date (UND)

Sites agree *not* to extend offers prior to a specified date and time

Uniform Acceptance Date (UAD)

Sites agree *to* extend offers prior to a specified date and time

Note – some sites set their own timelines and do not adhere to either the UND or the UAD!

Singularity – Does APPIC and APA accreditation matter? Not really! In contrast to internship, APPIC and APA accreditations are not as important at the postdoc level. Many forensic training sites do not pursue APPIC membership and the postdocs they offer are not APA-accredited. However, the experiences obtained through these postdocs still count toward the supervised hour requirements for licensure as a psychologist.

POSTDOCTORAL PARTICULARS

Due to similarities between the postdoc application process and the internship application process, the postdoc application process itself may feel familiar and repetitive to applicants. However, there are some important considerations in deciding whether to apply to a forensic postdoc, which sites to apply to, and which offers to accept.

How do I decide if I want a forensic postdoc? Possibly the most common reason that individuals apply for a postdoc is because it guarantees they will receive the supervised hours they need to be eligible for licensure as a psychologist in most jurisdictions (Forand & Applebaum, 2011). However, as noted above, supervised hours do not necessarily need to be obtained from a formal postdoc, so a consideration regarding whether to apply for postdoc is the personal appeal of entering the workforce. For many, finances are a primary motivating factor. If faced with heavy student loan debt, the appeal of earning more money in the workforce can be strong. However, student loans can be deferred during postdoc, which provides some financial relief, although interest may continue to accrue (Bailey, 2004b).

The potential applicant's training goals are another important consideration. Those who want to enhance their skills in a specific area often seek a postdoc to gain additional experience under the supervision of an expert in the field. For example, individuals pursuing a forensic postdoc may seek additional experience in forensic assessment. In graduate school or during internship, they may have had opportunities to conduct forensic psychological testing and assist in writing forensic reports, but during postdoc they may be responsible for conducting full forensic evaluations and maintaining an independent (but supervised) caseload. This also applies to individuals seeking re-specialization. For example, a neuropsychologist may have vast experience writing neuropsychological assessment reports, but little experience writing reports that address forensic questions. As such, individuals in non-forensic specialty areas may seek additional training via a postdoc to help them re-specialize their skillsets.

Career goals are another vital consideration in deciding whether to apply for a postdoc. For example, to become board certified in forensic psychology by the American Board of Professional Psychology, candidates must accumulate at least 100 hours of specialized forensic training and 1,000 hours of direct forensic clinical experience over a minimum of 5 years post-graduation (American Board of Professional Psychology, n.d.). These requirements may be most efficiently satisfied via completion of a forensic postdoc.

Another common career goal that can be served by a postdoc is the development of a professional network in a specific geographic region. The structure of a formal postdoc program, which often includes inter-acting with a range of forensic psychologists beyond the trainee's primary supervisor, can help ease the transition to becoming an autonomous professional, forge professional connections, and open up job opportunities. Completing a postdoc can open opportunities specifically in academics. Research postdocs provide experience with writing grants and publishing articles, which makes the individual more attractive for a faculty position (Pelham, n.d.). Alternatively, for future academics who want to engage in clinical practice on the side, satisfying licensure requirements by completing a postdoc may prove to be a shrewd move. Although it is possible to negotiate supervised work experience in academic settings, gaining supervised work hours while teaching may be a less efficient pathway towards fulfilling licensure requirements than delaying academic aspirations for 1 year and completing a postdoc (Walton, 2014).

A final consideration in deciding whether to complete a postdoc is career flexibility. In the field of psychology, remaining in one position for the entirety of one's career is the exception rather than the norm. Professionals often change jobs; it is not uncommon for practicing clinicians to look for a change of scenery in an academic setting or for fatigued academics to seek refuge in clinical practice. Postdocs can further both academic and clinical careers, so those looking for career versatility may contemplate completing a postdoc. Additionally, completing a postdoc provides flexibility in both career path and location. Those unsure of where they would like to settle or who enjoy frequent changes of scenery might rest easier knowing they are completing a formalized program of supervised work hours (Walton, 2014).

How do I decide to which sites to apply? There are several considerations when narrowing down your postdoc site list. A key consideration is the number of sites to which to apply. Unlike internship, where applicants often apply to 10–15 sites, postdoc applicants often apply to fewer sites. The reduced number of applications may stem from several factors, including formal postdocs not being a necessity for licensure, reduced competition due to a smaller applicant pool, and a smaller number of sites from which to choose.

Another consideration is a desire for board certification. The American Board of Forensic Psychology (ABFP) requires psychologists to have practiced for at least 5 years and gained some forensic experience before applying for board certification as a forensic psychologist. Realistically, completion of any forensic postdoc can place a psychologist on the path to board certification, but some sites expressly address board certification in their training and may offer didactic seminars focused on forensic assessment practices and relevant case law. Training at some of these postdoc sites allows for a waiver of the 5-year waiting period required by ABFP if the site adheres to certain guidelines and is approved by ABFP.

Board certification (discussed in Chapter 9) offers several benefits, including widely recognized expertise in forensic psychology. For psychologists considering board certification, applying to postdoc sites that meet ABFP requirements for the experience waiver can expedite the board certification process.

Training sites that offer forensic internships may also offer forensic postdocs. There are several advantages to applying for a postdoc at the site where you are completing internship. First, the internship site has already provided you with some training and likely has a sense of your strengths, areas for improvement, and potential as a psychologist. Second, although the statistical odds may not technically shift any more in your favor, having a pre-existing relationship with a site is one factor that can weigh positively in your favor, assuming you made a good impression. Third, you do not have to relocate if your postdoc is completed at the same site where you completed your internship.

As with most things, there may also be potential downsides to completing a postdoc at the same site where you completed internship. First, it may limit opportunities to expand your professional network. The field of forensic psychology is relatively small, so working with different individuals

ABFP WAIVER GUIDELINES

(American Board of Forensic Psychology, 2014)

- Provide a structured written curriculum with didactic training offered internally
- Provide at least 2,000 hours of training, with at least 25% of those hours spent in direct clinical service
- Provide at least 2 hours of face-to-face supervision per week
- Maintain a process of written evaluation documenting training progress and encompassing a trainee's strengths and weaknesses

who have different connections will expand your professional connections. Second, it may limit growth opportunities. Forensic psychologists can avoid complacency and continue to develop by gaining exposure to new supervisors, professionals, and organizations with different ways of thinking and practicing. If a goal of postdoc is to expand your professional horizons, then completing a postdoc at a different site from where you completed your internship may be the best course of action.

A final consideration concerns training goals. Like internships, forensic postdocs vary widely in terms of experiences offered and populations served. Some postdocs are research and policy focused and may act as stepping stones to future academic careers, while others are clinically focused and may facilitate a career in public or private clinical practice. Still others are blended, offering primarily a research experience or a clinical experience, but with some time dedicated to both activities. Postdocs vary in terms of forensic populations served. For example, some postdocs might offer a specialized track in sex offender risk assessment, while others might focus predominantly on questions of competence to stand trial and criminal responsibility. Still others might offer opportunities to conduct civil forensic evaluations. Finally, some postdocs are more networking-oriented than others. For example, some programs encourage fellows to attend professional conferences or multi-day forensic training workshops.

How do I decide which offer to accept? Considerations regarding which offer to accept are based largely on the sites to which an individual applies. Common considerations include the salary, geographic location, experiences offered, and access to desired professional networks. The range of salaries across postdocs is quite large, with some sites offering no salary and others offering highly attractive compensation packages.

For some, the biggest determinant of which offer to accept is fit with the site. The concept of fit encompasses some aspects discussed earlier in this chapter, such as how well the site matches an individual's training goals, but it also includes how comfortable you feel at the site and how well you got along with staff with whom you interviewed. Another fit-related consideration is expectations regarding the training level of applicants. Some postdocs are geared more towards individuals with minimal previous exposure and therefore focus on skill acquisition, while others expect that individuals already have a substantial amount of experience. Therefore, fit with the site's training approach is an important consideration in making the experience fulfilling and professionally rewarding.

A final consideration when deciding which offer to accept is the reputation and prestige of the site. Forensic psychology is still an emerging subfield of psychology. Sites with training staff who are renowned in the field of forensic psychology can be attractive, both in terms of the credibility of one's training and in terms of gaining exposure to individuals who have crafted the field and helped drive it forward.

FELLOWSHIP FILL-INS

Although postdocs are the final formalized pathway to obtaining forensic specialization, there are other options for obtaining forensic training after completing graduate school. Four common options include obtaining a job in a forensic or related setting, attending continuing education (CE) seminars, pursuing re-specialization, and obtaining forensic supervision.

As indicated earlier in this chapter, some choose to enter the workforce after graduation instead of completing a postdoc. Specialized training in the form of a forensic postdoc can help someone to obtain a job in a forensic or related setting (e.g., correctional or neuropsychology setting), but it is not a necessity. The general clinical skills obtained during graduate school and internship are translatable and may sufficiently prepare someone for a career as a correctional psychologist, unit psychologist at a state hospital, or psychologist in private practice.

Certain jobs in forensic or related settings can effectively serve as informal postdocs. Some jurisdictions allow individuals awaiting licensure to work as an "associate" or "resident," or to work under a temporary license ("Psychologist Licensing Process," n.d.), which permits them to practice psychology under the supervision of a licensed psychologist. However, unlike a formal postdoc, informal postdocs may not have a formal training structure or offer didactics.

Another postgraduate option for pursuing specialization includes completing CE credits. Many institutions offer forensic seminars that fulfill CE requirements (Ogloff, Tomkins, & Bersoff, 1996). These seminars vary widely from a single 3-hour session offering a brief overview of a forensic psychology topic to full-day or multi-day workshops that provide highly detailed and in-depth information.

CONTINUING EDUCATION CREDITS

Most jurisdictions require the completion of continuing education (CE) credits on a regular basis to maintain licensure as a psychologist.

Forensic psychology is not always the first love of professional psychologists, but this interest may emerge later in one's career. For these individuals, postdocs can be used to re-specialize. However, for those uninterested in a formal postdoc, a school-based re-specialization program is an option for obtaining postgraduate training in forensic psychology. A handful of graduate schools offer graduate certificate programs in forensic psychology, which require completion of a small number of courses relevant to forensic specialization. These programs specifically target individuals with a terminal graduate degree in psychology or a related subfield. Of note, they do not require completion of a supervised training experience.

A final postgraduate pathway to obtaining specialized forensic training is contracting for supervision with a forensic psychologist. This option might be ideal for those with a variety of transferable skills or those looking to gain exposure to forensic psychology without making it their primary practice area. For example, a school psychologist who receives a referral with legal relevance may contract with a forensic psychologist to supervise the case and help him or her navigate the additional considerations associated with forensic mental health assessments.

★ ★ ★

CONCLUSION

Postdocs are typically 1–2-year post-graduate training positions focused on specialization in a subfield of psychology. For aspiring forensic psychologists, postdoc may be a sound option for those looking to gain novel specialized training or for those looking to master an existing forensic skillset. Unlike internship, postdocs are not a required part of psychology training (unless one is specializing in neuropsychology). Notable similarities to the internship process include requirements for supervision by a licensed psychologist, search strategies to identify sites, and application materials and timelines, while notable differences include the lack of a match system and less emphasis on sites being accredited by APPIC or APA.

In deciding whether to pursue a postdoc, important considerations include:

- a plan to pursue board certification;
- desired forensic experiences; and
- enhancing one's CV to be more competitive in the job market.

In deciding which offer to accept, common considerations include:

- salary, geographic region, and access to desired professional network;
- forensic experiences offered;
- fit with the site; and
- reputation of the site and its training staff.

For those who elect to forgo postdoc and enter the workforce, specialized forensic training can be gained in other ways after graduate school, including jobs in a forensic (or related) setting, continuing education seminars, re-specialization, and contracting with a forensic psychologist for supervision.

REFERENCES

American Board of Forensic Psychology. (2014, September 18). *Experience waiver and postdoctoral training in forensic psychology guidelines.* Retrieved on June 6, 2019 from www.abpp.org/BlankSite/media/Forensic-Psychology-Documents/ABFP-Experience-Waiver-Postdoc-Training-Guidelines.pdf

American Board of Professional Psychology. (n.d.). *Specialty specific requirements.* Retrieved on June 6, 2019 from https://abpp.org/Applicant-Information/Specialty-Boards/Forensic-Psychology/Application,-Specialty-Specific-Fees.aspx

Bailey, D. S. (2004a, January). The skinny on the postdoc. *gradPSYCH Magazine.* Retrieved on June 6, 2019 from www.apa.org/gradpsych/2004/01/postdoc-skinny

Bailey, D. S. (2004b, September). Preventing premature loan repayment. *gradPSYCH Magazine.* Retrieved on June 6, 2019 from www.apa.org/gradpsych/2004/09/repayment

DeMatteo, D., Marczyk, G., Krauss, D. A., & Burl, J. (2009). Educational and training models in forensic psychology. *Training and Education in Professional Psychology*, *3*, 184–191.

Forand, N. R., & Applebaum, A. J. (2011). Demystifying the postdoctoral experience: A guide for applicants. *The Behavior Therapist*, *34*(5), 80–86.

How to find a postdoc. (2014, April). *gradPYSCH Magazine*, *12*(2), 36. Retrieved on June 6, 2019 from www.apa.org/gradpsych/2014/04/postdoc-search

Kuo, P. (2012, July/August). Four ways to find a postdoc. *Monitor on Psychology*, *43*(7), 76. Retrieved on June 6, 2019 from). www.apa.org/monitor/2012/07-08/postdoc

Novotney, A. (2017, February). Postdoc opportunities abound, if you know where to look. *Monitor on Psychology*, *48*(2), 58. Retrieved on June 6, 2019 from). www.apa.org/monitor/2017/02/postdoc-opportunities

Ogloff, J. R. P., Tomkins, A. J., & Bersoff, D. N. (1996). Education and training in psychology and law/criminal justice: Historical foundations, present structures, and future developments. *Criminal Justice and Behavior*, *23*, 200–235.

Pelham, B. (n.d.). *Doing postdoctoral work—should I?* Retrieved on June 6, 2019 from www.apa.org/careers/resources/academic/postdoc-work

Psychologist Licensing Process. (n.d.) Retrieved on June 6, 2019 from www.psychologist-license.com/articles/psychologist-licensure.html

Walton, A. G. (2014, April). To postdoc or not to postdoc? *gradPSYCH Magazine*, *12*(2), 35. Retrieved on June 6, 2019 from). www.apa.org/gradpsych/2014/04/postdoc

CHAPTER 9

Practice Qualifications

As you may have realized by this point in the book, becoming a forensic psychologist is a long process. Before graduate school even starts, those interested in forensic psychology need to ensure they have the right type of education, training, and experience to be competitive for a doctoral program, and then they need to identify graduate programs that are a good fit and apply to those programs (see Chapters 3, 4, and 5). Graduate training itself can last 2–7 years, depending on the type of program (e.g., master's program, doctoral program, joint-degree program) (see Chapters 6 and 7). After earning a doctoral degree, some students choose to pursue a 1- or 2-year postdoctoral fellowship to obtain additional clinical experience and advanced specialization (see Chapter 8).

After all of the education and training that culminates in earning a doctoral degree, surely you must be ready to practice as a forensic psychologist, right? Well, not quite yet. The practice of forensic psychology is governed by laws and regulations, so some additional credentials are needed before you can engage in the independent practice of forensic psychology. In addition to legal and regulatory oversight of the profession, forensic psychology is governed by several ethics codes. In this chapter, we focus on the laws, regulations, and ethics that govern the practice of forensic psychology.

BECOMING LICENSED

As you may remember from Chapter 1, we endorsed a broad definition of forensic psychology that includes both applied components (i.e., evaluation and treatment) and research components. Conceptualizing forensic psychology in this inclusive manner acknowledges the many contributions that can be made to the United States legal system by psychologists working in both clinical and research capacities. This definition of forensic psychology is also consistent with the definitions endorsed by leading psychology organizations, including the American Psychological Association (APA) and the American Board of Forensic Psychology (ABFP).

Although both clinical psychologists and research psychologists working at the intersection of psychology and law can be appropriately conceptualized as forensic psychologists, clinical forensic psychologists must satisfy additional requirements before they can engage in the independent practice of forensic psychology. Specifically, forensic psychologists who engage in clinical practice, such as the assessment and treatment of criminal offenders or civil litigants, must be licensed as psychologists. By contrast, forensic psychologists who exclusively conduct research are not required to be licensed because they are not providing direct services to the public.

Clinical psychology (which includes clinical forensic psychology) is one of many professions that requires its practitioners to be licensed. There are some obvious professions that require licensure in most states, including accountants, chiropractors, dentists, lawyers, optometrists, physical therapists, physicians, pilots, real estate agents, and veterinarians. But many states also require licenses for acupuncturists, auctioneers, barbers, cemetery salespeople, cosmetologists, crane operators, massage therapists, midwives, natural hair braiders, and timeshare salespeople. Licensure of these professionals is governed by state administrative boards, with the purpose of protecting the public by ensuring that members of these professions meet certain minimum standards indicative of competent practice.

There is an important distinction between licensure and certification (see Slobogin, Hafemeister, Mossman, & Reisner, 2014). Although both mechanisms are intended to protect the public, the means by which they accomplish that goal differ. Licensure limits the performance of certain activities or the provision of certain services to a designated class of people, and it also limits the use of certain professional titles (e.g., psychologist, physician). As we will see, states restrict the acquisition of a psychologist's license to those who meet established qualifications and satisfy certain procedural requirements. An alternative to licensing used in some states is certification (sometimes called "title licensing"). Certification restricts the use of certain titles to those who meet specified training and experience requirements. In summary, licensing limits the performance of certain activities and titles to those who have a license, while certification only limits the use of specific titles. For example, in states that use certification, people cannot call themselves "psychologists" unless they meet certain requirements. However, certification does not restrict activities, which means people can engage in activities typically associated with psychology, such as counseling, as long as they do not refer to themselves as a psychologist.

Currently, all 50 states require psychologists to be licensed by the state(s) in which they practice, and some states have both licensure and certification of psychologists. Interestingly, the requirement that psychologists be licensed is relatively new, and several states did not require licensure until relatively recently. There are various steps to becoming licensed as a psychologist, and a discussion of licensure requirements can be complicated because states have different requirements for who is eligible to become licensed and what psychologists must do to obtain a license. There are, however, some websites that provide concise summaries of licensure requirements across all states, including a site maintained by Psychologist-License.com (see Psychology Licensing Process, n. d.). Also, some states, including Massachusetts and Virginia, require those who practice forensic psychology to obtain a specialty certification.

Despite variations in psychologist licensure laws across states, most states have similar requirements. States typically specify requirements for licensure in administrative regulations enacted by the state board of psychology, and these regulations can be enforced by courts if a practitioner violates them. In general, individuals are eligible to be licensed as psychologists if they earned a doctoral degree from an accredited program, amassed a sufficient number of supervised practice hours, passed one or more standardized tests, completed necessary paperwork, and paid required fees. Once these requirements are met, they become licensed psychologists who are qualified for independent clinical practice in a particular jurisdiction.

Education

As a starting point, most states require a doctoral degree for the practice of psychology, but there are some exceptions worth noting. For example, until relatively recently, most states permitted those with master's degrees to practice as school psychologists. When the laws in those jurisdictions changed and began requiring a doctoral degree, the existing school psychologists with master's degrees were "grandfathered in," which means they were permitted to continue practicing as school psychologists without obtaining a doctoral degree; the doctoral-degree requirement only applied prospectively to new school psychologists entering the profession. Further, in some states, individuals with master's degrees can use the title "psychologist" in certain settings. In general, though, a doctoral degree is considered the entry-level degree for the independent practice of psychology.

As briefly noted in Chapter 4, most states require that candidates for licensure earn their doctoral degree from a program accredited by the APA. Graduates of programs not accredited by APA can still become licensed in some states, but the process is more complicated. APA accreditation of a doctoral program provides assurance to a state licensing board (e.g., State Board of Psychology) that the program meets certain basic requirements related to the curriculum and training. APA accreditation is a "stamp of approval" indicating that the program is of sufficient quality to train aspiring psychologists who will be capable of competent independent practice. Some states also require that candidates for licensure complete an APA-accredited internship, although most states only require graduation from an APA-accredited doctoral program. Graduates of non-APA-accredited doctoral programs may be asked to provide some assurance that their training was of sufficient breadth, depth, and quality to qualify them for licensure. In those instances, candidates may need to provide course descriptions, letters from training directors, or other indicators of the training they received.

Supervised Practice Hours

All states require that candidates for licensure as a psychologist obtain a specific minimum number of supervised practice hours before being eligible for licensure; supervised practice hours are accumulated when students obtain real-world experience (e.g., assessment, therapy) under the supervision of a licensed professional. Some states require the accumulation of supervised hours both before and after the receipt of a doctoral degree. Candidates for licensure typically can satisfy the predoctoral supervised hours requirement through their internship; most APA-accredited internships are designed to provide psychology interns with enough supervised hours to qualify them for licensure. In states that require postdoctoral supervised hours, candidates for licensure may choose to complete a postdoctoral fellowship (see Chapter 8) or some other supervised experience to obtain a sufficient number of hours.

There is considerable variation among states in terms of the number and types of hours that count towards licensure. For example, in Pennsylvania, candidates for licensure need 1 year of postdoctoral supervised experience, with 1 year defined as a period of at least 12 months and consisting of at least 1,750 supervised hours. There are a number of restrictions related to acceptable hours in Pennsylvania: no more than 45 hours but no less than 15 hours of experience can be counted in a given week, the required hours must be obtained within 10 years from award of the doctoral degree, all experience must be supervised, and 50% of the required hours must be obtained by performing diagnosis, assessment, therapy, other interventions, supervision or consultation, or by receiving supervision or consultation; the remaining hours can be obtained through teaching, research, or a variety of other activities specified in the licensing regulation. By contrast, Florida requires 4,000 hours of supervised experience, although up to 2,000 hours accumulated during a predoctoral internship may be counted towards the total hours.

Standardized Tests

All states require candidates for licensure as a psychologist to take the Examination for Professional Practice in Psychology (EPPP), which is a national licensing exam designed by the Association of State and Provincial Psychology Boards (ASPPB) (Association of State and Provincial Psychology Boards, 2019). The EPPP is computer-administered at official testing sites throughout the United States. The current version of the EPPP consists of 225 multiple-choice questions, with 175 of the questions counting towards the score and the remaining 50 questions being tested for potential inclusion in a future version of the test. Test-takers have 4 hours and 15 minutes to complete the exam, which translates into answering roughly one question per minute. The EPPP covers eight domains thought to be essential to psychological practice: biological bases of behavior; cognitive-affective bases of behavior; social and cultural bases of behavior; growth and lifespan development; assessment and diagnosis; treatment, intervention, prevention, and supervision; research methods and statistics; and ethical/legal/professional issues. There are four equivalent versions of the EPPP, and every 6 months one form is discontinued and another form is introduced.

The results of the EPPP are available immediately to test-takers. EPPP scaled scores range from 200 to 800, and most states require a passing score of at least 500, which is equivalent to answering approximately 70% of the questions correctly (Association of State and Provincial Psychology Boards, 2019). If a test-taker fails, he or she can retake the test, but states vary in terms of how long a test-taker must wait to do so and how many total times a candidate can take the EPPP; however, in all states, no one is permitted to take it more than four times in a 1-year period. Also, in some states, individuals are eligible to take the EPPP as soon as they earn their doctoral degree, while other states require candidates for licensure to obtain the required supervised hours before being permitted to take the EPPP.

A new version of the EPPP – the Enhanced EPPP – is under development and scheduled to be available in all jurisdictions in January 2020 (Association of State and Provincial Psychology Boards, n.d.a). The Enhanced EPPP will include two parts. EPPP Part 1, which is the current multiple-choice exam, is designed to assess psychological knowledge, while EPPP Part 2 will be a new addition designed to assess psychological skills. States will not be required to adopt the Enhanced EPPP and can choose to continue to use to the current EPPP. EPPP Part 2 was developed to enhance a state licensing board's ability to assess a candidate's readiness for independent practice.

In addition to the EPPP, some states require candidates for licensure to pass a state-specific examination. Whereas the EPPP focuses broadly on psychological knowledge, state exams typically cover state-specific laws, regulations, and ethical standards. In Pennsylvania, for example, candidates for licensure must take the Pennsylvania Psychology Law Exam (PPLE) after they pass the EPPP. The PPLE consists of 30 multiple-choice questions on Pennsylvania law and ethics. Test-takers are given 1 hour to complete the exam, and they must answer at least 75% of the questions correctly to pass the test.

In addition to the EPPP and perhaps a state-specific test, some states require candidates for licensure to pass an oral examination. The oral exams differ across states. For example, in some states, the oral exam functions as the state-specific test, and candidates are tested on relevant laws, regulations, and ethics. In other states, candidates are presented with clinical vignettes or required to submit practice samples that form the basis of the oral exam, which focuses more on psychological knowledge relevant to clinical practice.

Paperwork and Fees

As with most applications, there is a variety of paperwork that needs to be submitted as part of the licensure application. In addition to providing basic background information, most state licensing boards request academic transcripts, verification letters from doctoral program directors (indicating that the candidate successfully completed all doctoral requirements from an APA-accredited program), official test scores, verification of postdoctoral experience (indicating that the candidate completed the required number of supervised practice hours), candidate evaluations completed during the course of postdoctoral supervision, and a letter from the postdoctoral supervisor (attesting to the candidate's readiness to practice psychology). There are, of course, fees associated with almost every step in the licensure process, including fees for taking the standardized tests and submitting the licensure application for review.

Miscellaneous Requirements

In addition to the requirements noted above, some states have other requirements for licensure as a psychologist. For example, some states require documented assurance that the candidate has acceptable character and reputation. To satisfy this requirement, states may require submission of a fingerprint-based criminal background check and child abuse history clearance. Some states may also require the applicant to submit reference letters that specifically address the applicant's character. These sources of information assist state psychology boards in determining if a candidate is fit to be an independent licensed psychologist in that jurisdiction.

As previously noted, there is considerable variation among states in terms of the requirements for licensure as a psychologist, so it is a good idea to familiarize yourself with the licensure requirements in your jurisdiction. With that said, there is certainly no pressing need to check the licensure requirements for those of you who are in graduate school; in fact, many graduate students are likely unfamiliar with the specific licensure requirements in their jurisdiction. However, a quality, APA-accredited graduate program will prepare students for the variety of licensure requirements seen across states. Once again, this highlights the importance of carefully choosing a graduate program.

REQUIREMENTS FOR LICENSURE AS A PSYCHOLOGIST

- Education (typically a doctoral degree in psychology or a related field)
- Supervised hours
- Examination for Professional Practice in Psychology (EPPP) and often state-specific tests
- Paperwork and fees

Licensed Psychologist!

As a licensed psychologist, you can engage in the independent practice of psychology. You can conduct assessments, provide therapy, and offer consultation, and no one must supervise you to make sure you are doing things correctly. Licensure is recognition by the state that you are qualified for the independent practice of psychology; you are an autonomous professional who can practice psychology with no oversight (although you must adhere to the relevant legal, regulatory, and ethical provisions in your state). Those with master's degrees in psychology can sometimes conduct evaluations or provide therapy – even if they are not licensed – but they cannot do so independently and must be supervised by a licensed professional, such as a licensed psychologist. Those who are Licensed Professional Counselors (LPCs), which is a credential available in some states, can function independently, but it would be rare for an LPC to be hired to perform a forensic evaluation. In the forensic arena, most lawyers and courts seek to work with professionals who have the highest degrees available in their field.

Licensed psychologists must maintain their license in good standing. Psychologists must renew their license every year or every other year (depending on the state). Besides paying a fee, license renewal typically involves affirming you have not been subject to an ethical complaint or lawsuit based on professional misconduct, and most states require psychologists to earn a minimum number of continuing education (CE) credits in the time period since the previous license renewal. In Pennsylvania, for example, licensed psychologists must complete 30 hours of CE every 2 years, including at least 3 CEs in ethics, 2 CEs in child abuse recognition and reporting, and 1 CE in suicide prevention. There is variation among states in terms of what activities satisfy CE requirements, but psychologists in many states can obtain CE credits by attending approved seminars or workshops, teaching college courses, publishing articles and book chapters, and taking quizzes after reading select articles.

BOARD CERTIFICATION

Congratulations! You gained admission to graduate school in a highly competitive environment, completed the arduous graduate training, earned your doctoral degree, and satisfied all requirements for licensure. You are officially a licensed psychologist – an independent professional who can work in a variety of employment settings. You can now conduct forensic assessments, provide therapy, and consult with attorneys, correctional facilities, government agencies, and a variety of other entities and organizations. Surely, there is nothing else you need to do to demonstrate your expertise in forensic psychology, right? Assuming you received the proper education/training and obtained your license, there is technically nothing more you need to do to practice as a forensic psychologist. However, forensic psychologists interested in demonstrating heightened expertise may choose to pursue board certification. Licensure is an indication by the state that a professional meets a minimum standard of competence, but board certification is an indication that a professional has achieved a heightened level of expertise.

There are various boards that offer certification for forensic psychologists, but the oldest and most respected is the American Board of Professional Psychology (ABPP). ABPP was incorporated in 1947 and it functions as the governing body of separately incorporated specialty examining boards (American Board of Professional Psychology, n.d.). Currently, psychologists can obtain board certification from ABPP in 15 specialty areas. Each of the 15 boards has separate requirements for becoming certified in that area.

ABPP SPECIALTY AREAS

- Behavioral and cognitive
- Clinical
- Clinical child and adolescent
- Clinical health
- Clinical neuropsychology
- Counseling
- Couple and family
- Forensic
- Geropsychology
- Group
- Organizational and business
- Police and public safety
- Psychoanalysis
- Rehabilitation
- School

Psychologists who choose to become board certified in forensic psychology must complete a rigorous application process that typically takes 1–2 years. Board certification in forensic psychology is overseen by the ABFP, which is one of the 15 specialty boards under the umbrella of

ABPP. ABFP was established in 1978 to protect consumers of forensic psychological services by (a) establishing, promoting, and revising the standards and qualifications for those who practice forensic psychology, and (b) providing certification of qualified psychologists. There are several steps to becoming board certified in forensic psychology by ABFP.

Application and Credential Review

The process of board certification is initiated by the submission of a general application to ABPP. The candidate must first demonstrate that he or she satisfies the generic requirements for board certification established by ABPP, and then demonstrate that he or she also satisfies the specialty-specific requirements for the specific board through which certification is being sought. To become board certified in any of the 15 specialty areas, all candidates must meet the following general eligibility requirements:

- (For those who obtained their doctoral degree prior to 2018) A doctoral degree – PhD, PsyD, or EdD – from a program in professional psychology that is accredited by the APA or Canadian Psychological Association, or from a program listed in the publication "Doctoral Psychology Programs Meeting Designation Criteria" (Association of State and Provincial Psychology Boards, n.d.b). Candidates who hold a Certificate of Professional Qualification in Psychology, which is provided by the Association of State and Provincial Psychology Boards (ASPPB), are deemed to satisfy this first requirement.
- A recent change is that candidates who obtained their doctoral degree in 2018 or later from a program in the United States or Canada must have been awarded their doctoral degree from a program that was accredited by the APA, Canadian Psychological Association, or an accrediting agency recognized by the U.S. Department of Education at the time of their graduation.
- Candidates must be licensed as psychologists (at the doctoral level) for the independent practice of psychology in a jurisdiction in the United States, a United States territory, or Canada.

In addition to satisfying these generic requirements, ABFP requires candidates for certification in forensic psychology to satisfy the following criteria:

- The candidate must have accrued at least 100 hours of qualifying specialized training in forensic psychology after the completion of the doctoral degree; *and*

• The candidate must demonstrate sufficient experience in forensic psychology after the completion of the doctoral degree by either (a) accumulating 1,000 hours of direct experience in forensic psychology over a minimum of 5 years, or (b) completing a full-time (minimum of 2,000 hours) formal postdoctoral training program in forensic psychology that has been accepted as meeting ABFP's training requirements. For candidates with a law degree, the 5-year period is reduced to 3 years, but the requirement of obtaining 1,000 hours of direct forensic experience must still be met.

Written Examination

Candidates who pass the general and specialty-specific credential review are permitted to take the written exam. Currently, the closed-book written exam consists of 197 multiple-choice questions, which must be answered in 3.5 hours, and it assesses the breadth of the candidate's forensic knowledge in seven areas:

1   ethics, guidelines, and professional issues;
2   law, precedents, court rules, civil and criminal procedures, and judicial practices;
3   testing and assessment, examination issues, and application of scientific knowledge to legal procedure;
4   civil competence, individual rights and liberties, workplace discrimination, and employment rights;
5   juvenile, parenting, and family/domestic/matrimonial matters;
6   civil damages, personal injury, disability, and workers' compensation; and
7   criminal competence and criminal responsibility.

A candidate must meet three criteria to pass the written exam: (1) correctly answer at least 70% of the questions; (2) correctly answer at least 60% of the questions in all seven categories; and (3) correctly answer at least 70% of the questions in six of the seven categories. Candidates get three chances to pass the written exam. If the candidate does not pass on the first try, a second attempt may be made no earlier than 6 months and no later than 18 months after the candidate received the results of the first exam. If a candidate does not pass the written exam on the second try, a third attempt may be made no earlier than 6 months and no later than 18 months after the candidate received the results of the second exam. If a candidate fails the exam a third time, the candidacy is terminated, and the candidate must wait at least 1 year before reapplying.

Practice Sample Review

Candidates who pass the written exam must submit two practice samples that will be used as the basis for the oral exam (discussed next). Practice samples are typically two forensic reports written by the candidate as part of his or her forensic practice. The practice samples must be in two distinct areas of forensic psychology, which allows the candidate to demonstrate expertise in multiple areas. Each practice sample consists of an introduction, forensic report, all test protocols, and supplementary materials the candidate chooses to include (e.g., relevant laws in the candidate's jurisdiction, case-specific criminal justice records, court orders).

The practice samples are thoroughly reviewed by at least two ABFP-certified forensic psychologists. If deemed acceptable, the candidate proceeds to the oral exam. If only one of the practice samples is deemed acceptable, the candidate must submit a replacement practice sample within 6 months (or the candidacy is terminated). If both practice samples are deemed unacceptable, the candidacy is terminated, and the candidate must wait at least 1 year before submitting two new practice samples.

Oral Examination

The final step in the ABFP board certification process is the oral exam. Oral exams are scheduled within 3–9 months following approval of the candidate's practice samples. The 3-hour oral exam is conducted by three ABFP-certified forensic psychologists. Candidates who successfully pass the oral exam officially become ABFP-certified forensic psychologists. Candidates who are not successful at the oral exam stage must submit two new practice samples and be prepared to retake the oral exam.

ABFP REQUIREMENTS FOR BOARD CERTIFICATION IN FORENSIC PSYCHOLOGY

- Application and credential review
- Written examination
- Practice samples review
- Oral examination

Final Notes

Unlike some other professions, becoming board certified in forensic psychology is not the norm. Most physicians, for example, are board certified in their specialty area, but less than 5% of psychologists become board certified by the ABPP. As of this writing, there are less than 400 ABFP-certified forensic psychologists listed in the ABFP directory, despite large numbers of psychologists who engage in forensic practice. There are, however, various efforts to increase the number of board certified forensic psychologists, so we anticipate that more psychologists will choose to demonstrate their heightened expertise through board certification in the coming years.

A Word of Warning: There are several boards that offer certification in forensic psychology without any rigorous review or examination process; these so-called "vanity boards" often only require that psychologists have an active credit card to cover the certification fee. In exchange, psychologists receive a certificate documenting board certification status and can advertise themselves as being board certified. The problem, however, is that board certification from these types of boards does not signify heightened expertise and does not protect the recipients of the psychologist's services, which are the two primary functions of board certification. Hopefully as consumers, attorneys, and courts become more educated about board certification, these vanity boards will be eliminated.

ETHICAL PRACTICE

As noted earlier in this chapter, the practice of psychology is governed by a variety of laws, regulations, and ethics. Having discussed the laws and regulations relevant to the practice of psychology in the previous sections, we turn our attention to the general and forensic-specific ethical guidelines that govern the field.

Ethical Principles of Psychologists and Code of Conduct

The *Ethical Principles of Psychologists and Code of Conduct* ("*Ethics Code*") is the general ethics code published by the APA (American Psychological Association, 2017). APA published the first version of the *Ethics Code* in 1952, and it has been revised approximately 10 times since then, with the most recent revisions occurring in 2016 (with an effective date of

January 1, 2017). The *Ethics Code* applies to all APA members and APA student affiliates; psychologists who are not members of APA are not governed by the *Ethics Code* unless the *Ethics Code* has been adopted into state law by the state in which they practice.

The *Ethics Code* provides broad guidance to psychologists in fulfilling their roles as scientists, educators, supervisors, therapists, and evaluators, and it also seeks to protect those with whom psychologists work, including students, clients, research participants, and the general public (American Psychological Association, 2017). The *Ethics Code* consists of a Preamble, General Principles, and Ethical Standards. The Preamble describes the goals of psychologists and introduces the remainder of the *Ethics Code*. The General Principles are aspirational, which means they are not enforceable, but instead reflect the highest standards of the field. This highlights an important distinction – "guidelines" are aspirational and "standards" are enforceable. The Ethical Standards are the more specific and enforceable rules that address a variety of domains, including competence, human relations while functioning in a professional role, privacy and confidentiality, public statements, record keeping and fees, education and training, research and publication, assessment, and therapy. Although there is a section of the *Ethics Code* pertaining to forensic activities, the ethical guidance is not specific enough to address the unique ethical challenges that arise in forensic contexts.

Specialty Guidelines for Forensic Psychology

To provide more specific guidance to forensic psychologists, APA adopted the *Specialty Guidelines for Forensic Psychology* ("*Specialty Guidelines*") in 2011 (and published them in 2013). The current iteration of the *Specialty Guidelines* is an update of the *Specialty Guidelines for Forensic Psychologists*, which was published in 1991 by the Committee on Ethical Guidelines for Forensic Psychologists. The *Specialty Guidelines* was developed as a complement to the *Ethics Code* to provide ethical guidelines that are more specific to the practice of forensic psychology.

The *Specialty Guidelines* specifies the conduct expected of psychologists who engage in the practice of forensic psychology, which it broadly defines in a manner that is consistent with the one endorsed in this book. The *Specialty Guidelines* consists of an Introduction, a description of the *Specialty Guidelines*' purpose and scope, and ethical guidelines that address forensic psychologists' responsibilities for their conduct and services, competence, relationships with the parties they serve, confidentiality and privilege, methods and procedures in providing services, and public/ professional communications.

As guidelines (not standards), the *Specialty Guidelines* was intended to provide aspirational (not enforceable) guidance for the practice of forensic psychology. In fact, the *Specialty Guidelines* states that they "are not intended to serve as a basis for disciplinary action or civil or criminal liability" (American Psychological Association, 2013, p. 8). However, some states have adopted the *Specialty Guidelines* into state law, which means that psychologists in those jurisdictions can be held responsible if they fail to adhere to requirements in the *Specialty Guidelines*.

Other Ethical Guidance

The *Ethics Code* and *Specialty Guidelines* are the two most broadly applicable ethics codes, but several more specific ethics codes have been developed. For example, (APA 2010) adopted the *Guidelines for Child Custody Evaluations in Family Law Proceedings* ("*Child Custody Guidelines*") in 2009 (and published them in 2010). In recognition of the unique and complex issues involved in child custody evaluations, the *Child Custody Guidelines* provides guidance for conducting child custody evaluations. As with the *Specialty Guidelines*, the *Child Custody Guidelines* is intended to be aspirational, although some states have made it enforceable by adopting the *Child Custody Guidelines* into state law. There is also an ethics code that applies to psychiatrists who engage in forensic practice. The *Ethical Guidelines for the Practice of Forensic Psychiatry* ("*Ethical Guidelines*") was published by the (American 2005) Academy of Psychiatry and the Law in 2005. Much like the *Specialty Guidelines* applicable to forensic psychology, the *Ethical Guidelines* was developed to address the unique ethical concerns faced by forensic psychiatrists.

REGULATION OF PSYCHOLOGISTS

We have discussed licensure and certification as ways to screen unqualified practitioners from the field and protect the public from substandard services. These mechanisms function prospectively to prevent the public from being harmed. There are several other mechanisms that protect the public from subpar care provided by psychologists, including forensic psychologists. Specifically, there are three sources of authority that can be used to hold psychologists accountable for substandard work and address the concerns of those who believe they have been harmed by a psychologist: professional organizations, state licensing boards, and state law.

Professional Organizations

Psychologists who are members of professional organizations must adhere to the ethics code adopted by those organizations. For example, as noted, all APA members must adhere to the (APA 2017) *Ethics Code*. Psychologists who are bound by the *Ethics Code* can be sanctioned by APA if it is determined that the psychologist deviated from expected behavior. After receiving a complaint from an aggrieved recipient of services, APA can institute an investigation into the psychologist's behavior. The investigation is strictly governed by a number of procedural rules designed to make the process fair to all parties.

If the APA Ethics Committee determines that a psychologist has violated an enforceable provision of the *Ethics Code*, the psychologist can be subject to several types of sanctions, including a reprimand, censure, expulsion from APA, or required resignation from APA; the nature of the sanction is based on the severity of the psychologist's misconduct. The psychologist may also be required to stop engaging in certain activities, only practice under supervision, receive additional training or education, be evaluated and/or receive treatment (e.g., mental health, substance abuse), or serve a period of probation (i.e., strict monitoring of the psychologist's practice for a specified period of time).

State Licensing Boards

The practice of psychology is governed by each state, typically by a state board of psychology responsible for the licensing and oversight of psychologists. To that end, state boards enact regulations that govern the behavior of psychologists in that jurisdiction. Given their oversight role, state boards can impose sanctions on psychologists who violate the administrative regulations. There are, however, limits on the available sanctions. State boards cannot impose jail time or order monetary restitution, but they can impose fines and restrict the ability of a psychologist to practice in that state. In instances involving egregious conduct by a psychologist, the psychologist can permanently lose his or her license to practice psychology in that state. When choosing a psychologist, consumers can check the state board of psychology website in their state to see if the psychologist has ever been sanctioned for unethical conduct.

State Law

If a consumer of psychological services believes he or she has been harmed by a psychologist's unprofessional conduct, the injured party can sue the psychologist for malpractice. A malpractice action typically involves an allegation that a psychologist was negligent in providing professional services. Malpractice actions against psychologists are similar to malpractice actions against other professionals (e.g., medical malpractice). To prevail in the malpractice suit, the injured party (plaintiff) must show four things: (1) the professional had a duty recognized by law to conform to a certain standard of conduct; (2) the professional failed to meet the required standard; (3) the professional's conduct directly harmed the plaintiff; and (4) the plaintiff suffered damages (e.g., missed work, worsening mental health) (see Slobogin et al., 2014). Plaintiffs who succeed in malpractice suits can be awarded money to compensate them for their harm and punish the psychologist for providing negligent care.

★ ★ ★

CONCLUSION

Being a psychologist is a privilege that comes with both rights and responsibilities. As a specialty area of psychology, forensic psychologists are – first and foremost – psychologists who must meet certain practice standards and adhere to general ethical guidelines. However, as discussed throughout this book, the practice of forensic psychology differs from traditional psychological practice in several ways. The recent development of ethics codes specifically applicable to forensic psychology is recognition that forensic psychology is a distinct area of practice and that forensic psychologists need forensic-specific guidance to fulfill their roles.

Of note, forensic psychologists often work with disadvantaged and disenfranchised populations of criminal offenders who may be facing severe legal consequences, with vulnerable civil litigants who have suffered some psychological and perhaps physical injury, or with offenders in forensic psychiatric hospitals experiencing the effects of severe mental illness. The oftentimes high-stakes legal contexts in which forensic psychologists conduct evaluations or provide therapy highlight the importance of ensuring that psychologists are properly trained, licensed/certified by the state, and adherent to applicable ethical guidelines and standards.

REFERENCES

American Academy of Psychiatry and the Law. (2005). *Ethics guidelines for the practice of forensic psychiatry*. Bloomfield, CT: Author. Retrieved on July 20, 2019 from www.aapl.org/pdf/ethicsgdlns.pdf.

American Board of Professional Psychology. (n.d.). About ABPP. Retrieved on July 20, 2019 from www.abpp.org/About.aspx.

American Psychological Association. (2010). Guidelines for child custody evaluations in family law proceedings. *American Psychologist, 65*, 863–867.

American Psychological Association. (2013). Specialty guidelines for forensic psychology. *American Psychologist, 68*, 7–19.

American Psychological Association. (2017). *Ethical principles of psychologists and code of conduct.* Washington, DC: Author. Retrieved on July 20, 2019 from www.apa.org/ethics/code/ethics-code-2017.pdf.

Association of State and Provincial Psychology Boards. (2019, January). *EPPP candidate handbook.* Retrieved on July 20, 2019 from cdn.ymaws.com/www.asppb.net/resource/resmgr/eppp_/eppp_cand-handbook-1_16_2019.pdf.

Association of State and Provincial Psychology Boards. (n.d.a). *EPPP part 2 information.* Retrieved on July 20, 2019 from www.asppb.net/page/EPPPPart2.

Association of State and Provincial Psychology Boards (n.d.b). ASPPB/National Register designated doctoral programs in psychology historical listing (1981-2018). Retrieved on September 4, 2019 from https://cdn.ymaws.com/www.asppb.net/resource/resmgr/mobility_/asppb_national_register_desi.pdf

Committee on Ethical Guidelines for Forensic Psychologists. (1991). Specialty guidelines for forensic psychologists. *Law and Human Behavior, 15*, 655–665.

Psychology Licensing Process. (n.d.). *Psychology licensing process.* Retrieved on July 20, 2019 from www.psychologist-license.com/articles/psychologist-licensure.html.

Slobogin, C., Hafemeister, T. L., Mossman, D., & Reisner, R. (2014). *Law and the mental health system: Civil and criminal aspects* (6th ed.). St. Paul, MN: West Publishing Co.

FURTHER READING

Bartol, C. R., & Bartol, A. M. (2018). *Introduction to forensic psychology: Research and application* (5th ed.). Thousand Oaks, CA: SAGE Publications.

Brigham, J. C. (1999). What is forensic psychology, anyway? *Law and Human Behavior, 23*, 273–298.

Costanzo, M., & Krauss, D. (2018). *Forensic and legal psychology: Psychological science applied to law* (3rd ed.). New York: Worth Publishers.

Huss, M. T. (2014). *Forensic psychology: Research, clinical practice, and applications* (2nd ed.). Hoboken, NJ: John Wiley & Sons.

CHAPTER 10

The World Is Your Oyster

Jobs and Professional Development

It has been a long road. You are now a forensic psychologist. You completed your education, training, and perhaps became licensed (if you practice clinical forensic psychology), and you may even be board certified by the American Board of Forensic Psychology. What now? At various points throughout this book, we described some of the employment options available to forensic psychologists, but it is time for a more in-depth discussion. This brings us back to one of the first questions we addressed in this book: What do forensic psychologists do?

This chapter focuses on the various jobs and employment contexts in which forensic psychologists can work. As you will see, forensic psychologists possess a unique and highly marketable skillset that makes them qualified for many different jobs in a variety of settings. We also examine relevant considerations for early-career professionals in forensic psychology, such as getting involved in professional organizations and keeping abreast of the latest developments in the field. Given the pace at which the field of forensic psychology is evolving, it is important for forensic psychologists to be familiar with ways to keep up to date with new developments.

JOBS FOR FORENSIC PSYCHOLOGISTS

Most people spend approximately one-third of each weekday working at their job, so it is important to choose a job that checks multiple boxes for you. If you created a wish list for a job, it might include a variety of considerations. For example, before accepting a job, you might consider the following factors (in whatever order is most desirable to you): job responsibilities, job satisfaction, pay and benefits, geographic location, job security, the ability to maintain a work–life balance, and the opportunity for career advancement. The good news is that, with the advanced education and training that come along with being a forensic psychologist, there are numerous jobs that would satisfy these (and other) considerations. We cannot possibly discuss every job available to forensic psychologists, so we will instead focus on the categories of jobs that are most relevant (see Bartol & Bartol, 2019).

Academia

Some forensic psychologists are employed as professors at a college or university. Given their training, forensic psychologists are typically based in departments of psychology, but it is not uncommon for forensic psychologists to be in other departments, including criminology and criminal justice. A few forensic psychologists are primarily (or secondarily) affiliated with a law school, particularly if they have training in both psychology and law. As professors, forensic psychologists teach courses, conduct research (if trained to do so), publish, and likely sit on a variety of committees (department, college, university, and professional). Some institutions focus more on teaching as opposed to research, particularly smaller teaching colleges, but larger colleges and universities tend to focus on both teaching and research. Ideally, the courses they teach, research they conduct, and publications they produce will be in the field of forensic psychology. Professors sometimes teach classes that are not related to forensic psychology, either because they have diverse professional interests or there is no one else in the department who is a better fit to teach the course. Similarly, forensic psychologists may conduct research that is not related to forensic psychology. Again, some forensic psychologists have diverse research interests and enjoy being involved in non-forensic research. Another possibility is that research funding may not be readily available in their areas of interest, so they seek grants (which are important for career advancement in academia) in non-forensic research areas that are more likely to be funded by state and federal agencies.

In academic settings, forensic psychologists who are not clinically trained focus primarily on conducting research that can be used to inform some aspect of the justice system. We described some of the research conducted by forensic psychologists in Chapter 2. Forensic psychologists who are clinically trained may choose to integrate forensic assessments into their work at the college or university. For example, some graduate programs have a forensic clinic through which graduate students can gain professional experience assisting with forensic assessments under the supervision of the forensic psychologist. Other forensic psychologists in academic positions operate a private forensic practice or become part of an existing group practice. These set-ups are often win–win situations for both the forensic psychologist and his or her students. The professor can engage in an enjoyable activity that potentially pays very well, and the students are able to build their forensic skillset and begin networking with professionals with whom they might work after completing their graduate training.

Academic salaries vary considerably based on a variety of factors, including geography, setting, and academic rank. For example, salaries tend to be higher in larger metropolitan areas where there is a higher cost of living. Professors in departments of education tend to make higher salaries than those in departments of psychology, criminology, or criminal justice, and those based in law schools typically make higher salaries than those in colleges of arts and sciences (in which many psychology departments are housed). Forensic psychologists in an academic medical setting, such as a department of psychiatry at a medical school, tend to make considerably more money than psychologists employed in colleges of arts and sciences. However, psychologists in academic medical settings may receive "soft money," which means their entire salary is not guaranteed; in these contexts, they may be expected to earn 50% or more of their salary through grants, contracts, or providing clinical services.

A recent salary survey conducted by the American Psychological Association's Center for Workforce Studies provides some insight into the salaries psychologists make in academic settings (Christidis, Lin, & Stamm, 2018). The College and University Professional Association for Human Resources (CUPA-HR) survey gathered data from nearly 240,000 full-time faculty members at 696 U.S. colleges and universities. Here are the main takeaways from the survey with respect to psychology professor salaries during the 2017–18 academic year:

- The median salary of a tenured full professor of psychology at U.S. doctoral universities was $114,259. [According to the Carnegie Classification of Institutions of Higher Education, doctoral universities are institutions that award at least 20 research/scholarly doctoral degrees per year.]

ACADEMIC TENURE

A tenured professor has an indefinite academic appointment that can only be terminated for cause or extraordinary circumstances (e.g., financial emergencies).

- The median salary of a tenured full professor of psychology at U.S. baccalaureate colleges was $82,247. [According to the Carnegie Classification of Institutions of Higher Education, baccalaureate colleges are institutions where (a) bachelor's degrees account for at least 10% of all undergraduate degrees and (b) fewer than 50 master's degrees are awarded per year.]

DID YOU KNOW?

Professors at colleges and universities come in three ranks:
- Assistant professor
- Associate professor
- (Full) professor

- The median salary of a new tenure-track assistant professor of psychology at U.S. doctoral universities was $73,350.
- The median salary of a new tenure-track assistant professor of psychology at U.S. baccalaureate colleges was $55,364.
- Across different ranks and schools, tenured psychology professors earned a median salary of $88,977, tenure-track associate professors earned $71,586, and tenure-track assistant professors earned $62,031.

There are various ways to slice the CUPA-HR survey data, and a few other points are worth noting. Overall, psychology professors made less than professors in most STEM (Science, Technology, Engineering, and Medicine) and social science disciplines. The salary discrepancy with other disciplines has been exacerbated because salary levels for psychology professors have stagnated over the past few years. Also, as previously noted, geography matters. The survey found that psychology professors in the Pacific region (Alaska, California, Hawaii, Oregon, and Washington) earned the highest median salaries, while faculty in the West South Central region (Arkansas, Louisiana, Oklahoma, and Texas) and West North Central region (Iowa, Kansas, Minnesota, Missouri, Nebraska, North Dakota, and South Dakota) earned the lowest salaries (Christidis et al., 2018). Psychology faculty at private academic institutions made more money (median $98,637) than psychology faculty at public academic institutions (median $88,906) or private religious institutions (median $84,827) (Christidis et al., 2018).

The CUPA-HR survey also provided salary data based on the race/ethnicity and sex of psychology professors (Christidis et al., 2018). Racial- and ethnic-minority faculty are underrepresented in psychology departments. For example, the survey revealed that only 17% of tenured/tenure-track associate professors and 11% of full professors were racial or ethnic minorities. With that said, racial- and ethnic-minority faculty earned 4–8% more than their White counterparts. In terms of sex, although women outnumbered men among assistant and associate psychology professors, men outnumbered women (56% vs. 44%) among full professors, which is the highest academic rank. Finally, across all academic ranks, tenured/tenure-track women made slightly less money than tenured/tenure-track men: female full professors earned a median of $88,848 compared with $90,934 for men, female associate professors earned $70,908 compared with $73,188 for men, and female assistant professors earned $62,004 compared with $62,671 for men.

Academic positions offer a number of benefits that may be attractive to forensic psychologists, including a flexible schedule, the opportunity to teach forensic psychology courses and conduct forensic psychological research, opportunities for collaborating with internal and external colleagues who share similar professional interests, working with students interested in forensic psychology, conducting forensic assessments and providing consultation, and job stability (particularly if the faculty member is tenured). The potential for supplementing one's academic income with money earned performing forensic work (e.g., assessments, consultation) is also attractive, although schools have varying policies regarding how much "extra" compensation faculty members are permitted to earn.

Private Practice

Another career option for forensic psychologists is private practice. This could involve being a sole proprietor or working in a group practice with other forensic psychologists. There are numerous activities that can be performed by forensic psychologists in private practice. They could, for example, limit their practice to conducting forensic assessments, or perhaps they want to conduct assessments and also provide consultation. Some may choose to be affiliated with a college or university as an adjunct professor who occasionally teaches a course or conducts research, while others may maintain their private practice while also moonlighting in other settings (e.g., providing community mental health counseling, working 1 day per week in a correctional facility). Some private practitioners actively publish and become involved in professional organizations. To refresh your memory about these various activities, you might want to flip back to Chapter 2, which discusses the types of forensic assessments that can be conducted, the types of consultation that can be provided, and the nature of forensic psychological research.

Working in private practice as a forensic psychologist has several benefits. The freedom associated with being your own boss is attractive to many forensic psychologists. As a solo practitioner and perhaps in some group practices, forensic psychologists set their own working hours, establish their own payment rates, and limit their activities to what they want to do. Although generating business may be a challenge for early-career professionals or for forensic psychologists who relocate to a new geographic area, there are typically many opportunities to expand a private forensic psychology practice.

Another attractive aspect of private practice is the compensation. Most insurance companies do not reimburse for the cost of a forensic assessment (because they are not conducted for treatment-related purposes), which means forensic psychologists can set their own rates without having to worry about being reimbursed by a third-party payor. The rates and fee schedules used by forensic psychologists vary. When conducting a forensic assessment, the fees forensic psychologists charge are determined by a number of factors, including the amount of time that will be needed to complete the evaluation (i.e., review the file, conduct the evaluation, score the tests, write the report), whether deposition or court testimony will be needed, and the geographic location (with larger metropolitan areas typically being associated with higher fees). With that said, psychologists are free to charge whatever fees the market can withstand.

There are a variety of fee structures. Some forensic psychologists prefer flat rate agreements in which the psychologist receives a set amount of compensation regardless of the number of hours expended; this type of arrangement may be attractive to attorneys who retain forensic psychologists and are looking to contain costs. Flat fees for forensic assessments can range from several hundred to several thousands of dollars. Other forensic psychologists prefer charging by the hour. Again, there is considerable variation, but hourly fees could easily fall in the $200–500 range, with more experienced forensic psychologists being able to charge higher rates. Some forensic psychologists charge one rate for the evaluation and a separate fee for testimony, with the latter fee potentially being an additional several hundred or several thousand dollars.

In smaller markets or for forensic psychologists with little experience, it may be challenging to charge high rates, but the potential to earn $200,000+ per year is certainly possible. A 2014 report from the American Psychological Association noted that experienced forensic psychologists in private practice often earn between $200,000 and $400,000 annually. Although forensic psychologists can typically set their own rates and use a variety of fee structures, they are prohibited from using contingency fee arrangements in which the psychologist's compensation is a percentage of the monetary award received by the plaintiff; this type of arrangement could compromise the psychologist's objectivity because tailoring the report so that the plaintiff receives a larger monetary award would directly financially benefit the psychologist. Finally, some forensic psychologists believe that conducting pro bono (i.e., no-cost) or low-cost (sometimes called low bono) forensic assessments is an important service to provide, particularly for criminal offenders or civil litigants who cannot afford the standard cost associated with a forensic assessment.

Forensic psychologists can also charge money for providing consultation to attorneys, courts, correctional facilities, treatment facilities, social service agencies, departments of behavioral health, and other entities and organizations. As with forensic assessments, the most common fee structures for forensic consultation are flat fees or hourly rates. There is also considerable variability with consultation fees, but the potential to make a very comfortable living is certainly realistic once the psychologist gains experience and establishes his or her professional reputation.

Correctional Facilities

Some forensic psychologists work in correctional settings, such as jails and prisons. An important distinction we have touched on several times throughout this book is the difference between forensic psychology and correctional psychology. There is some obvious overlap between these professions in terms of educational requirements (typically a doctoral degree), credentialing (requires a license if providing human services), skillsets (primarily assessment, treatment, and consultation), and the populations with whom they work (typically criminal offenders), but forensic psychology and correctional psychology should be viewed as distinct professions (see Neal, 2018). Although this book is focusing on forensic psychology, we will briefly discuss correctional psychology because of its overlap with forensic psychology.

DID YOU KNOW?

Although often used interchangeably, there are important differences between **jails** and **prisons**. **Jails** hold individuals who have been charged with an offense and are awaiting trial, or offenders who have been convicted and sentenced to a short term of incarceration (typically less than 2 years, although it differs by jurisdiction). By contrast, **prisons** are for offenders who have been sentenced to longer terms of incarceration.

As we noted in Chapter 1, there are various definitions of forensic psychology, so it should not be surprising that there are also varying definitions of correctional psychology, along with some disagreement on the nature and degree of overlap between forensic psychology and correctional psychology. As a reminder, we define forensic psychology as the application of scientific, technical, or other specialized knowledge of psychology to inform matters within the judicial system, legislative bodies, and administrative agencies. Psychologists from any specialty area (e.g., clinical, developmental, social, cognitive) can engage in forensic psychology. By contrast, correctional psychology is "a subfield of psychology in which basic and applied psychological science or scientifically oriented professional practice is applied to the justice system *to inform the classification, treatment, and management of offenders to reduce risk and improve public safety*" (Neal, 2018, p. 652). As with forensic psychology, any type of psychologist can be considered to be engaging in correctional psychology if he or she applies the "scientific, technical, or specialized knowledge of psychology to reduce offender risk and improve public safety" (Neal, 2018, p. 652).

Besides definitional differences, forensic psychology and correctional psychology operate in different domains and at different points in the legal process. Forensic psychology is often involved during the (pre-) adjudication process before the court makes a final determination in a case. As discussed throughout this book, forensic psychologists may evaluate criminal offenders or civil litigants to help courts address a specific legal question (e.g., competence to stand trial, insanity, psychological damages, child custody), present relevant research to the court to help the court make a determination, or provide restorative therapy to an offender who was determined to be incompetent to stand trial. By contrast, correctional psychologists are typically involved after the court has made a final determination in a criminal case. In that capacity, correctional psychologists may provide mental health treatment to inmates, conduct research on the effects of a violence reduction program, and assist correctional facilities to more effectively manage inmates. As may be evident, a key difference between forensic psychology and correctional psychology is that correctional psychology is typically not used to inform a specific legal decision.

Correctional psychologists may be employed in jails or prisons at the local, state, or federal level. The Federal Bureau of Prisons (BOP) has a widely respected internship program in several locations throughout the United States, and many students pursuing a career in forensic psychology complete the BOP internship to gain assessment and treatment experience with criminal offenders. There are nearly 7 million people under correctional supervision in the United States (Kaeble & Cowhig, 2018), so the demand for correctional psychologists will likely continue to increase, which makes it an attractive job option for those interested in working at the intersection of psychology and law. In terms of salary, correctional psychologists typically earn less than forensic psychologists who are employed in either an academic setting or in private practice, but correctional psychologists often enjoy stable work schedules, attractive benefits, and some level of job security.

State Forensic Hospitals

Forensic psychologists can be employed as staff psychologists at state forensic hospitals throughout the United States. These facilities vary in terms of the populations they serve, but state forensic hospitals can house patients in several categories, including individuals who have been civilly committed, offenders who have been determined to be incompetent to stand trial, and offenders who have been found not guilty by reason of insanity (see Chapter 2 for a refresher of these categories).

Forensic psychologists in state forensic hospitals can perform a variety of services centered around assessment and treatment. For example, forensic psychologists may conduct evaluations of civilly committed patients to see if they continue to meet the criteria for civil commitment – i.e., imminent danger to self or others, or substantially unable to care for themselves. Psychologists in these settings may also conduct evaluations of incompetent patients (to see if they are still incompetent) or provide restorative therapy to those patients to help them regain their competence so the legal process can resume. Forensic psychologists in state forensic hospitals may also be asked to provide testimony in court about their assessment results and their opinions on the legal issue being addressed by the court. As state employees, salaries are generally lower than what forensic psychologists earn in most academic settings or in private practice, but the benefits package and stable work hours may make state forensic hospitals attractive options.

Court Clinics

Forensic psychologists in court clinics perform many of the same functions as forensic psychologists in private practice, but they can also take on other roles. They may conduct mental health evaluations of children, adolescents, or adults at the request of the court, assist in the development or evaluation of court-based or community treatment programs, provide therapy to those served by the court, or serve as a consultant to the court on a variety of issues that are at the intersection of psychology and law. As a court employee, the forensic psychologist may be required to serve a variety of functions to help the court performs its job. For those interested in engaging in diverse job functions, a court clinic may be attractive.

Juvenile Detention/Treatment Centers

Forensic psychologists can also ply their trade in facilities that work exclusively with juvenile offenders. When a juvenile offender is adjudicated delinquent of committing a crime, the juvenile may be sentenced to a period of detention in a secure residential facility. Psychologists in those settings perform both forensic and quasi-correctional functions involving assessment and treatment. They may, for example, conduct periodic assessments of the juveniles to determine their likelihood of re-offending, or they may provide individual/group therapy to juveniles who are experiencing mental health symptoms or are addicted to substances. Working with juveniles requires specialized training that can be obtained in some graduate programs, internships, and postdoctoral fellowships. Juveniles may present with different treatment needs than adults, and psychologists who work with juveniles need experience with juvenile-specific assessment and treatment approaches.

Law Enforcement Agencies (Police Psychology)

Psychologists are increasingly being hired by local, state, and federal law enforcement agencies. In these positions, psychologists are typically involved in assessment, treatment, operational support, and organizational consultation (Bartol & Bartol, 2019). Some of the roles they perform include conducting screening/suitability assessments for law enforcement officers, conducting fitness-for-duty evaluations of law enforcement officers after a critical incident (e.g., discharge of service weapon), assisting police departments in determining ideal work schedules to maximize officer safety and efficiency, training police officers and other first responders (e.g.,

Emergency Medical Technicians) on how to work effectively with special populations they may encounter while on duty (e.g., mentally ill, drug-involved, veterans), hostage negotiation, and providing counseling to law enforcement officers and their families. Forensic psychologists may also be hired as consultants to law enforcement agencies. Police psychology, like correctional psychology, is often excluded from the umbrella of forensic psychology, but we included a discussion of police psychology because there is overlap between traditional forensic psychological practice and this branch of psychology.

Research-focused Careers

Forensic psychologists can conduct research in a variety of settings, but they can focus almost exclusively on research when working for non-profit organizations, research-focused entities, government agencies, and so-called think tanks (or organizations that provide guidance in a particular area). In these contexts, forensic psychologists often conduct research, or use the results of research, to inform practice or policy in a specific area (e.g., drug policy, criminal justice reform). Translating research into action is an important part of the work of some forensic psychologists.

Final Notes

As previously noted, this chapter focused on the major job categories in which forensic psychologists can work, but there are many others we have not discussed. One of the benefits of having a doctoral degree is that many of the skills that are acquired throughout the many years of education and training are useful in multiple settings. The potential transferability of skills presents forensic psychologists with numerous job opportunities in both public and private sectors. Data gathered from members of the American Psychology-Law Society (AP-LS) revealed a diversity of employment settings for forensic psychologists, with 43% working in private practice, 25% in academia, 12% in hospital and other human services settings, and 10% in government positions (Griffin, 2011). The survey data are from 2011, so it is reasonable to assume that more recent data would reflect an even greater variety of employment.

In recent years, increasing numbers of forensic psychologists are creating their own jobs that involve a combination of the roles discussed above. For example, a forensic psychologist may be primarily based in an academic setting (either full-time or part-time), but also maintain a private forensic psychology practice. Other forensic psychologists are primarily self-employed, with a dual focus on forensic assessments and consultation. Some forensic psychologists primarily maintain a private practice, but also work part-time for a correctional facility or court clinic. Other forensic psychologists are self-employed as independent contractors for several agencies and organizations. Given the increasing recognition of the value of forensic psychology, we anticipate that forensic psychologists will be in even higher demand in the coming years, which will provide additional job opportunities.

JOB OPPORTUNITIES FOR FORENSIC PSYCHOLOGISTS

- Academia
- Private practice
- Correctional facilities
- State forensic hospitals
- Court clinics
- Juvenile detention/treatment centers
- Law enforcement agencies
- Research institutes/organizations

PROFESSIONAL DEVELOPMENT

Being a competent forensic psychologist requires engaging in ongoing professional development. Among other benefits, professional development helps forensic psychologists to maintain and enhance their knowledge and skills. An important aspect of professional development is staying current with new developments in the field. Forensic psychology is a rapidly growing and ever-evolving profession, which makes it challenging to remain current in terms of knowledge and skills. Forensic psychology is a profession that requires its practitioners to keep up with new developments in both psychology and law. Existing laws sometimes get overturned, new laws are being enacted with some regularity, courts are constantly issuing new decisions, ethics guidelines and standards occasionally get revised, new psychological tests are developed, and research is being published at a historically high rate. If forensic psychologists do not keep up with these changes, the field can easily pass them by, leaving them with outdated knowledge, a skillset that does not reflect current standards and best practices, and an incomplete understanding of the field. A related aspect of professional development is increased involvement in editorial, writing, and leadership roles, all of which can further one's career and contribute to the development of the field of forensic psychology. Fortunately, as will be discussed, there are several effective ways to keep pace with the changes that occur in forensic psychology and increase one's involvement in the field.

Professional Journals and Other Publications

Professional journals are regularly published periodicals that contain the most recent research being produced in a particular topic area. The substantial increase in forensic psychological research that occurred in the mid-1970s led to the development of several journals that are relevant to forensic psychology. As mentioned in Chapter 2, there are many professional journals that publish empirical, theoretical, and practice articles relevant to forensic psychology (e.g., *Behavioral Sciences and the Law; Criminal Justice and Behavior; International Journal of Forensic Mental Health; Law and Human Behavior; Psychology, Public Policy, and Law*). Some of these journals are published monthly, while others are published three, four, or six times per year. Some of these journals have a broad focus, while others are much more targeted. Routinely reading, or at least skimming, professional journals is an effective way to learn about new research and practice developments in forensic psychology.

A potential barrier is the cost of journals. Some journal subscriptions are several hundred dollars per year, which may make them cost-prohibitive. Fortunately, there are several ways to gain access to journals at little or no cost. Most college libraries carry several print or electronic versions of journals related to forensic psychology, which provides ready access to these publications for interested students. Also, as will be discussed, joining a professional organization often comes with a complimentary subscription to the organization's journal.

Besides journals, there are hundreds of books and Internet resources (e.g., websites, blogs) on forensic psychology (or the closely related field of forensic psychiatry). Some books are part of an established book series (e.g., Oxford University Press's Best Practices in Forensic Mental Health Assessment, AP-LS Book Series), while other books are stand-alone. Some books are so well regarded that they are considered staples of the field (e.g., *Handbook of Forensic Psychology* [Weiner & Otto, 2014]; *Principles of Forensic Mental Health Assessment* [Heilbrun, 2001]; *Psychological Evaluations for the Courts* [Melton et al., 2018]). The content in books is typically not as current as the content in journals (due to the frequency with which journals are published), but books can provide much more in-depth coverage of the material. Also, journals typically publish articles focusing on research, whereas books publish a much wider range of content.

If you become established as a forensic psychologist who conducts research and publishes articles, you may be asked to serve as a reviewer for a journal. As discussed in Chapter 6, manuscripts submitted to scientific journals undergo a peer-review process in which the manuscript is reviewed by several reviewers who have expertise in the specific topic area. Manuscripts that are favorably reviewed become published, while manuscripts with less favorable reviews are rejected or need to be revised before a publication decision is made. Rejection is the norm for most journals, and the more competitive journals have rejection rates of over 80%. Being asked to review a manuscript submitted to a journal is a sign that you are well regarded for your expertise. Reviewers who perform well – i.e., submit timely, detailed, insightful, and constructive reviews – may be asked to become a member of the journal's Editorial Board. For some journals, there may be several hundred reviewers, with Editorial Boards consisting of only 30–50 people. Being a journal reviewer or member of a journal's Editorial Board is a testament to one's reputation and expertise, and it can further your career, particularly for forensic psychologists in academia.

Professional Organizations

An effective way to remain aware of new developments is to become involved in a professional organization that focuses on forensic psychology (or the larger field of psychology–law). As mentioned in Chapter 2, there are several organizations for those interested in forensic psychology (e.g., AP-LS; Australian and New Zealand Association of Psychiatry, Psychology and Law; European Association of Psychology and Law; International Association of Forensic Mental Health Services). The eligibility requirements for these organizations differ, with some requiring an advanced degree and others being open to undergraduate and graduate students. The cost of membership also differs. Some organizations, such as AP-LS, are student-friendly; currently, students can join AP-LS for $15 per year.

DID YOU KNOW?

The American Psychological Association often writes legal briefs to appellate courts, including the Supreme Court of the United States. These briefs – which are called *amicus curiae* ("friend of the court") briefs – are intended to educate the court about the relationship between the law and some aspects of psychology.

There are several benefits to becoming a member of a professional organization. Membership in many of these organizations comes with a subscription to the organization's journal and/or newsletter. For example, all AP-LS members (including students) receive a complimentary subscription to the *AP-LS Newsletter* and the journal *Law and Human Behavior*, which is one of the premier psychology–law journals. Another benefit of membership is attending the organization-sponsored conferences. Organizational membership is not required to attend most conferences, but members are typically offered reduced conference registration rates, which can result in considerable cost savings. Conferences are typically held annually, and they serve as showcases for the latest research and developments in the field, so attending the conference is an effective way to keep abreast of the most recent updates. Attending conferences is also an opportunity to network with like-minded professionals. Conferences for larger organizations, like the American Psychological Association, routinely attract more than 10,000 attendees, while conferences for smaller, more-specialized organizations, like AP-LS, typically have approximately 1,000 attendees. Conversations with colleagues over coffee or a meal at a conference are a great way to establish collaborations and keep current with recent developments in the field.

Joining a professional organization also provides opportunities to obtain committee and leadership experience. Most professional organizations have a variety of committees that need to be staffed, and committee chairs are often looking for enthusiastic, young professionals to join the committee. After a few years of involvement with the organization, it may be possible to run for a leadership position (e.g., President, Treasurer, Secretary). These are all volunteer positions – not mandatory and typically unpaid – but they are a great way to increase your involvement in an organization, stay at the forefront of new developments, and give something back to the field by donating your time and expertise.

Continuing Education

Licensed psychologists are typically required to obtain continuing education (CE) credits to maintain their license in good standing with their state board of psychology. Besides being necessary to maintain their psychologist license, earning CE credits is an effective way for psychologists to stay current with recent developments in the field. As mentioned in Chapter 6, CE credits are available through many organizations, some of which are forensically focused, including the AP-LS, American Academy of Forensic Psychology, and Consolidated Continuing Education and Professional Training. CE seminars can address a variety of topics, but they typically focus on topics that are relevant to psychological practice (as opposed to research), given that only licensed psychologists (not experimental psychologists) are required to obtain CE credits. CE seminars might focus on general clinical topics, such as working with specific populations (e.g., children, adolescents, older adults, drug-involved clients, suicidal patients), new assessment approaches, clinical treatment strategies, and new developments in psychiatric medications. CE seminars can also focus on forensically relevant topics, such as working with criminal offenders, testing in forensic contexts, evidentiary standards for the admissibility of expert testimony, and many other topics. For convenience, CE seminars are offered in a variety of formats, including in-person, home-based study, webinars, and pre-recorded self-study.

PROFESSIONAL DEVELOPMENT IN FORENSIC PSYCHOLOGY

* Read professional journals and other publications
* Join professional organizations
* Participate in continuing education

★ ★ ★

CONCLUSION

Throughout this book, we hope we have conveyed our enthusiasm for the field of forensic psychology. Forensic psychology is an exciting, growing, and rapidly developing field, and forensic psychologists are engaging in important work in a variety of settings. For those interested in the intersection of psychology and law, the field of forensic psychology provides a wide range of opportunities, including assessment, treatment, research, consultation, and teaching. Given the anticipated growth of forensic psychology over the next few decades, we expect an increase in educational programs, training experiences, and job opportunities. For those readers who were unsure if forensic psychology is the right profession for them, we hope this book convinced you to seriously consider a career in this field. For those readers who were already interested in forensic psychology, we hope this book increased your desire to become a forensic psychologist. The field needs intelligent, hard-working, and passionate young professionals, so perhaps some of you will be among the next generation of forensic psychologists.

REFERENCES

American Psychological Association. (2014). *Pursuing a career in forensic and public service psychology.* Retrieved on July 21, 2019 from www.apa.org/action/science/forensic/education-training.pdf.

Bartol, C. R., & Bartol, A. M. (2019). *Introduction to forensic psychology: Research and application* (5th ed.). Thousand Oaks, CA: SAGE Publications.

Christidis, P., Lin, L., & Stamm, K. (2018, June). *Psychology faculty salaries for the 2017-2018 academic year: Results from the 2018 CUPA-HR survey of four-year colleges and universities.* Retrieved on July 21, 2019 from www.apa.org/work force/publications/18-faculty-salary.

Griffin, P. (2011, Winter). Presidential column. *American Psychology-Law Society News, 31* (1),2. Retrieved on July 21, 2019 from www.apadivisions.org/division-41/publications/newsletters/news/2011/01-issue.pdf.

Heilbrun, K. (2001). *Principles of forensic mental health assessment.* New York: Kluwer Academic Publishers.

Kaeble, D., & Cowhig, M. (2018, April). *Correctional populations in the United States, 2016.* Washington, DC: U.S. Department of Justice, Office of Justice Programs, Bureau of Justice Statistics. Retrieved on July 21, 2019 from www.bjs.gov/content/pub/pdf/cpus16.pdf.

Melton, G. B., Petrila, J., Poythress, N. G., Slobogin, C., Otto, R. K., Mossman, D., & Condie, L. O. (2018). *Psychological evaluations for the courts* (4th ed.). New York: Guilford.

Neal, T. M. S. (2018). Forensic psychology and correctional psychology: Distinct but related subfields of psychological science and practice. *American Psychologist, 73,* 651–662.

Weiner, I. B., & Otto, R. K. (2014). *Handbook of forensic psychology* (4th ed.). Hoboken, NJ: Wiley.

Index

Made in the USA
Coppell, TX
07 April 2023

15354182R00125